# REFUGEES & FORCED MIGRATION

**A Canadian Perspective**
*An A - Z Guide*

Catherine Baillie Abidi & Shiva Nourpanah

NIMBUS
PUBLISHING
—— NIMBUS.CA ——

Nimbus Publishing Limited
3660 Strawberry Hill St, Halifax, NS, B3K 5A9
(902) 455-4286 nimbus.ca

NB1404

Cover photo: *Immigrant children, 2005*. Oaxaca, Mexico, by Sylvia Calatayud
Design: Marlon Solis
Editor: Kate Juniper
Proofreader: Elizabeth Eve

Library and Archives Canada Cataloguing in Publication

Title: A Canadian perspective on refugees and forced migration : an A-Z guide /
    Catherine Baillie Abidi & Shiva Nourpanah.
Names: Baillie Abidi, Catherine, author. | Nourpanah, Shiva, author.
Description: Includes bibliographical references and index.
    Identifiers: Canadiana 20189068787 | ISBN 9781771087292 (softcover)
Subjects: LCSH: Refugees—Canada—Miscellanea. | LCSH: Refugees—Canada—
    Social conditions—Miscellanea. | LCSH: Forced migration—Canada—Miscellanea.
    | LCSH: Forced migration—Social aspects—Canada— Miscellanea. | LCSH:
    Canada—Emigration and immigration—Miscellanea. | LCSH: Canada—Emigration
    and immigration—Government policy—Miscellanea. | LCSH: Canada—
    Emigration and immigration—Social aspects—Miscellanea.
Classification: LCC HV640.4.C2 B35 2019 | DDC 325/.210971—dc23

Canada

Canada Council   Conseil des art
for the Arts     du Canada

NOVA SCOTIA

Nimbus Publishing acknowledges the financial support for its publishing activities from the Government of Canada, the Canada Council for the Arts, and from the Province of Nova Scotia. We are pleased to work in partnership with the Province of Nova Scotia to develop and promote our creative industries for the benefit of all Nova Scotians.

# Editors' Note

While refugees have been propelled into the spotlight in the past couple of years, particularly as a result of the Syrian crisis, historically they have never been far from public consciousness or policy debates.

As a result of these tensions, and emerging from years of close community and academic involvement in local, national, and international refugee affairs, we have identified a pressing need for a book that sets out basic terms and definitions in a politically aware and critically informed manner. As professionals in the migration landscape, our goal is to define key concepts in refugee affairs so as to educate and challenge settlement practitioners, policymakers, and interested members of the public, and to enhance understanding and awareness of policy and practice in this area.

*Refugees & Forced Migration: A Canadian Perspective* combines contributions of a passionate group of refugee activists, scholars, and practitioners, and the voices and perspectives of those with lived experiences of refuge. The result is a unique work that blends scholarship, activism, and refugee narratives to capture— as far as possible in such a work—the complex and multi-dimensional nature of the refugee experience.

*Refugees & Forced Migration* has been constructed within a critical theoretical framework that acknowledges Canada's complex history of human migration, and the evolution of exclusionary and racialized Canadian migration policies that have emerged in the process.

*—Catherine Baillie Abidi & Shiva Nourpanah*

# CONTENTS

# CONTENTS

# Historical Overview

## How the World Became Responsible for Protecting Refugees

### Marianela Fuertes

The thousands of displaced Syrians fleeing from a violent war in their country have provided the faces and the scenes that now shape much of the world's view of refugees. However, it was the aftermath of the Second World War that created the environment and conditions for the United Nations *Convention Relating to the Status of Refugees* to take place **(cf. 1951 Refugee Convention)**. The Second World War was the most deadly conflict in the history of humanity. Between 50 and 80 million people died during the six years of the war and millions more were forcibly displaced or expelled, setting the context for the origins of the international law for refugees and illustrating why humanity had to take action in the international context.[1]

The notions of human desirability and undesirability are evident throughout history. At the time of absolute monarchies, certain

---

[1]Today, Germany is taking a leading role in the Syrian refugee crisis and has received over 800,000 refugees. Perhaps these actions are inspired because Germany remembers the worst refugee crisis in Europe's history, when millions of people were forced to migrate, including the millions of Germans who were expelled from Eastern Europe during and after the war.

religions were persecuted and unwelcome in one state but were supported by powerful groups elsewhere. This was a process that increased throughout Europe during the sixteenth and seventeenth centuries, and which was reinforced by notions of national identity, eventually creating states defined by territory and a homogeneous identity under one sovereign. Borders closed in all senses—physically, politically, and economically—to guarantee the rise of powerful countries that then conquered and ruled the world. People were not allowed to move out or move in.

In such cases as the overthrow of monarchies through revolutions, the displacement of populations was for political reasons as well as religious. The French Revolution expelled twenty-five thousand members of the Catholic Church for refusing to swear fidelity to the new constitution. Others who came under any category of suspicion during the French Reign of Terror were persecuted, eliminated, or expelled with summary trials. The American Revolution, likewise, produced a chain reaction of displacement, expulsion, and persecution of all persons the new government perceived as opponents. It resulted in the displacement of five times more dissidents than that of the French reign of Terror.[2]

The consolidation of the nation as the identity of the state, in a world that was primarily shaped by a mercantilistic economy and colonial control, created constellations of stateless populations that were not recognized as part of an overarching national identity. This statelessness was further exacerbated by the application of the concept of **Citizenship (cf.)**, which meant that being a legitimate inhabitant was a condition only given by the authorities. In other words, only the citizens of the country

---

[2] Robert R. Palmer, *The Age of Democratic Revolution* (Princeton: Princeton University Press, 1959), 188.

have rights, while all others are aliens. This was the beginning of national minorities, and a stateless population crisis developed during the nineteenth century in those countries that produced the Industrial Revolution, and projected it later to their colonies during the twentieth century.

The First World War turned ethnically heterogeneous empires into ever-strengthening nation-states, which universalized the policy of a national constituent being defined as someone who is a part of the majority race. Consequently, minorities were seen as obstacles to the new regime. A person of different nationality needed special permission to be in the country. Only the nationals had the category of citizen and the right to be in the territory, with its defined and protected borders.

Categories of national identity only became more immutable over time since they were identified by ancestry. The circumstances of mono-national formula (when a nation is formed by a community of people with a common descent, language, culture, and history) made it impossible to convert in the way that religious adaptation was demanded by monarchies. The twentieth century saw the height of national homogenization, and during this process many people were left unable to adopt the majority identity because it was not about personal conviction or desire, but about ancestry and the place where you were born.

At the same time that borders were tightly guarded to inhibit the entry of "aliens," other borders became closed to those on the inside. The governments that emerged from the Russian Revolution closed Russia's borders to retain their population under an increase of authoritarian regimes that held thousands of people against their will, a practice that has since been adopted

by other illiberal regimes. Such policies were denounced as a violation of **Human Rights (cf.)** and this ideological discord was exploited as a political strategy during the Cold War, as western countries decried the oppression and created policies to encourage the migration of eastern European citizens that would enhance their professional working class and promote their dominant ideology of liberal democracy.

However, these policies that encouraged exodus from eastern Europe also had a counterpart, which was to strengthen the authority of the state to define what kind of immigrants they would like to accept. Western liberal countries were interested in skilled workers, yet they were not willing to accept the collective wave of minorities massively displaced as a result of the national identity construction. Pressures from native workers unwilling to accept the competition of foreign workers, whom they believed would undermine their livelihoods, further exacerbated the issue.

This ongoing dynamic between western and eastern countries— the former attracting skilled workers and the latter retaining people—has resulted in the great conceptual divide between **Refugees (cf.)** and immigrants **(cf. Migrant)** that now defines how countries manage the entry of foreigners.

The further refining of the immigration process led to a system that assigned quotas based not only on profession but on national origin. Thus, countries designed their immigration policies based on their political and ethical judgments, and these practices continue into the present.[3]

---

[3] Aristide R. Zolberg, *Escape from Violence: Conflict and the Refugee Crisis in the Developing World* (Oxford: Oxford University Press, 1989), 16.

These are the circumstances that have formed the basis of the immigration process in national sovereign states—and the background against which the international system for refugees has evolved. In the context of the emergence of nation states, the League of Nations created the High Commission to help address the influx of displaced Russians in Europe in 1921. The commission also assisted displaced peoples from Greece, Turkey, and Bulgaria—yet that office would end its mandate as soon as the populations it was assisting were resettled. Perhaps unsurprisingly, the commission was never able to complete its mandate, since the development of authoritarian regimes in other European countries continued, and so only increased mobilization, either by displacement or by resettlement. Thus, the commission was still operating after the Nazi Party's victory in 1933, which triggered the dramatic displacement of political opponents and Jewish citizens.

The Nazi regime caused an exodus of close to 2 million people in seven years, and in the wake of the resulting global crisis that worsened with the Great Depression, affecting all industrialized nations, in 1938 the League of Nations decided to create a permanent High Commission that would be responsible for all the League's work with refugees.[4] Under the organization of the League of Nations, countries agreed on a framework in which they were obligated to collectively respond to a crisis, create international organizations, and enforce a process of identifying and conceding refugee status to a person, based on political rather than economic reasons.

The job of the commission was quickly made impossible due to the lack of commitment from states to assume further responsibility for the refugee crisis, and yet the imperfect,

[4] Zolberg, *Escape from Violence*, 19.

Europe-focused approach to the global refugee crisis remains the foundation that informs how the international community handles refugee crises today.

In defining who would be considered a refugee and receive the assistance that the international community would be obligated to provide, the League agreed that the mere event of a person being displaced for political reasons must be considered insufficient because it could be applied to all people who lived under colonial regimes and therefore could give refugee status to too large a number of people: an undesirable consequence for the countries of the League of Nations.

The situation in Europe after the Second World War was by far the worst in modern times in terms of people displaced, famine, and destruction of the most basic social fabric. As multiple postwar surveys show, the total number of people displaced in the six years of the Second World War was around 30 million. Eleven million survivors remained outside their countries after the War and needed assistance.[5] Despite the number and the diverse composition of the displaced population (and the fact that it was hard to see a large number of these people as victims since their nationality related them to the Nazis), the process to resettle the majority of postwar refugees was completed in a short period of time.

In 1946 the International Refugee Organization (IRO) was established to complete the task of relocating the last of the refugees, who numbered around 1 million. The IRO's mandate

---

[5] Bernard Wasserstein, "European Refugee Movements after World War Two," *BBC*, last modified February 17, 2011, http://www.bbc.co.uk/history/worldwars/wwtwo/refugees_01.shtml.

would last until 1951 and then it would be dissolved. Amidst the tensions between member states who wanted to extend refugee status to displaced dissidents and anti-Communists and/or exclude those perceived as political enemies, the IRO advanced its major institutionalization process by distancing itself from the collective approach that had distinguished the High Commission's methods.

Instead the IRO took an individualized approach, founding the notion that the process to get refugee status must be the result of an individual application that would be processed by technical staff to determine if the applicant were eligible in accordance with the rule of the organization's mandate. These are the basic principles of the process that were reproduced by the United Nations High Commissioner for Refugees **(cf. UNHCR)**. Established in 1949 and with a mandate extended beyond displaced Europeans, with the exception of common and war criminals, UNHCR assumed responsibilities for a diverse group of populations in different regions of the world.

Since the institutionalization of an office that would work without regional restrictions and under technical rules, the main question for UNHCR and related bodies has become how to define who will get refugee status.

# 1951 Refugee Convention & the Protocol of 1967

## Marianela Fuertes

The 1951 Refugee Convention, also known as the United Nations *Convention Relating to the Status of Refugees*, was adopted by the UN General Assembly in 1951. It is grounded in Article 14 of the *Universal Declaration of Human Rights* **(cf. Human Rights)**, which recognizes the right of a person to seek **Asylum (cf.)** from persecution in other countries. The Convention entered into force on April 22, 1954, and it has since been the main international instrument for providing protection to **Refugees (cf.)**. It has only been subject to one amendment: the 1967 Protocol (in full, the *Protocol Relating to the Status of Refugees*), which changed the geographic and temporal limits of the Convention by granting it universal coverage in time and regions.

## ac·tiv·ism & ad·vo·ca·cy

# Gillian Smith

Canada has an international legal obligation to provide a system **(cf. Legislation)** whereby people fleeing persecution and asking for protection in Canada can go before an adjudicator and present their case. During the refugee claim process, a refugee claimant has a legal status **(cf. Status)** in Canada. They are issued a Refugee Protection Claimant Document (RPCD) by the federal government showing that they are a refugee claimant and therefore have rights, such as health coverage, under the Interim Federal Health Program (IFHP) **(cf. Health & Health Care)**.

And yet **Refugee Claimant (cf.)** status is often widely misunderstood—so much so that refugees themselves have become political pawns, since the laws and policies that deeply affect their lives and safety may change from one government to the next. Refugee claimants are continually at risk of being targeted by governments planning to renege on their rights and protection. Some leaders and political parties even campaign with the promise to do so, inciting xenophobia **(cf. Racism)** through anti-refugee rhetoric couched in populist rhetoric, as a result.

Consequently, advocacy and activism on an international, national, regional, and local level are vital and permanent practices in refugee matters in order to create and sustain legal rights and protections for refugees. Advocacy is not only necessary on the macro- or political level, but also on the micro- and meso-levels—the latter being the level within which the gatekeepers operate. These gatekeepers are front-line workers in a variety of services who have the power to include or exclude. Whether it is through lack of awareness, outright intention, or what can be labelled a "culture of no," front-line staff of various agencies may deny refugee claimants essential services and/or create confusion around eligibility. An example occurring on a local level is the medical receptionist who does not know how to process claims under the Interim Federal Health Program (IFHP), and so decides to deny refugee claimants access to medical services instead of exploring the issue. After all, it is often easier to say no than to complicate one's workday. While the focus of this entry is on illustrating exclusionary practices as a major reason for the continued need for advocacy, it would be remiss of me to not recognize the gatekeepers who do work hard to ensure access. These individuals are advocates too, and make positive impacts within generally oppressive structures.

Settlement support **(cf. Settlement Services)** for people making refugee claims is predominantly advocacy work. It shouldn't need to be, but it is. Providing settlement services requires advocating for, and more importantly with, the refugee claimant. It is necessary to emphasize *with*, since many definitions of advocacy use the preposition *for*—i.e. describing the action of advocating for a group—implying, intentionally or not, that the group has no agency and is unable to advocate for themselves. So the language that advocates use to express their cause can further oppress the group they seek to defend by promoting methods that serve to speak for groups, instead of with them. The national advocacy campaign "Walk with Refugees," a yearly march organized by the Canadian Council for Refugees, is a good example of how the name of a campaign creates a new narrative of advocacy, encouraging a form of advocacy that serves to flatten hierarchies and include people who are or were refugees as their own advocates. On a meso-level, walking with refugee claimants through daily challenges and supporting them to navigate complex systems often makes the difference between access and refusal, between inclusion and exclusion in areas such as health care, employment, and housing.

People making refugee claims are not helpless or passive recipients of support. They are often their own strongest advocate; but due to their precarious status, which marginalizes them in our society, and due to past experiences with government and perceived authorities, some might fear "rocking the boat" and so will be unwilling to speak up in situations where they are being denied services. Moreover, the Kafkaesque bureaucratic systems in Canada create a need for advocates familiar with its unnecessary complexities to anticipate upcoming **Barriers (cf.)** and act as brokers.

The ideal is that the role of the settlement worker, the broker, the advocate walking with refugees, should not need to exist. The reality is that advocates cannot rest, as any gains and progress made are sitting precariously close to the edge, in danger of being taken away, whether it be on micro-, meso-, or macro-levels, deliberately or unintentionally.

# A

a·sy·lum

## Marianela Fuertes

The practice of welcoming a foreigner who is fleeing **Persecution (cf.)** and providing them protection is an ancient concept that has existed for at least 3,500 years. The concept has been found in texts of ancient societies, including the following edict from a Hittite monarch: "Concerning a refugee, I affirm on oath the following: when a refugee comes from your land into mine he will not be returned to you. To return a refugee from the land of the Hittites is not right."[6] The Hittites were an ancient empire from 1600 BC. Likewise, the ancient Greeks, the Romans, and many contemporary nations make reference to their asylum practices: a power of the regent to guarantee protection to someone who is persecuted and deserves protection for political and humanitarian reasons. Asylum, also known as "sanctuary" in holy places, was often temporary, yet the practice itself became permanent as a prerogative of the state under sovereign decision.

During the process of writing the *Universal Declaration of Human Rights*, the founding members were very careful to establish the

---

[6] Darren O'Byrne, *Human Rights, An Introduction* (London: Routledge, 2013), 343.

right to seek asylum but not the right to get it—the *Universal Declaration of Human Rights* Article 14 (1) states: "Everyone has the right to seek and enjoy in other countries asylum from persecution."[7] In other words, every sovereign state has exclusive control over its territory and its decisions regarding the people allowed to be in it. The *Declaration on Territorial Asylum*, adopted by the General Assembly of the United Nations in 1967, Article 1(1) is worded thus: "Asylum granted by a State, in the exercise of its sovereignty, to persons entitled to invoke Article 14 of the *Universal Declaration of Human Rights* [...]". Article 1(2) states: "The right to seek and enjoy asylum may not be invoked by any person with respect to whom there are serious reasons for considering that he committed a crime [...]".[8]

These international instruments shape the conditions of asylum based on the sovereign decision of a state to guarantee asylum, rather than the right for the person to receive it. To seek asylum is an individual right, yet it is not clear to the asylum seeker who has the duty to provide it. However, the principle of not being forced to return **(cf. Non-refoulement)** prescribed in Article 33(1) of the 1951 Refugee Convention establishes the state's duty not to return an asylum seeker to a place where they have serious fears of being persecuted.[9] It is seen as a duty to guarantee protection against being returned to danger, even if the right of asylum is not guaranteed and the person may be sent somewhere else. It may

---

[7] UN General Assembly, *Universal Declaration of Human Rights* (10 December, 1948), http://www.un.org/en/universal-declaration-human-rights/.

[8] UN General Assembly, *Declaration on Territorial Asylum* (14 December, 1967), https://www.refworld.org/docid/3b00f05a2c.html.

[9] UN General Assembly, *Convention Relating to the Status of Refugees* (28 July 1951), https://www.refworld.org/docid/3be01b964.html.

be a weak protection, but this principle is the closest a person comes to having asylum as a right in international law.

bar·ri·ers

# Gillian Smith

The movement of people making refugee claims through systems and services in Canada is an exercise in patience and resilience as they navigate regional/provincial differences in access to services and overcome constant barriers. A person's immigration status **(cf. Status)**, or lack thereof, determines their rights, access to services, and inclusion in society—it opens or closes doors. People making refugee claims experience a poverty of status that is deliberate and that creates sweeping negative impacts on their lives.[10]

Imagine you had no right to work and had to wait for permission to do so, losing job opportunities while you struggled in poverty. Or you received large bills for essential health services, even though you were told you had health coverage, and thus became afraid to go to the hospital. Or you could not receive benefits for your children, even the ones who are Canadian citizens. Imagine you had to wait years to go before a judge whose sole decision will determine whether or not you and your family can stay in safety in Canada.

---

[10] It is important to point out that people with no immigration status experience the greatest poverty of status, making them vulnerable to egregious abuses, but this entry will focus on refugee claimants.

Those who possess **Permanent Residence (cf.)** and those who are citizens **(cf. Citizenship)** have a key that is often taken for granted; but it is a key that refugee claimants and those with certain other conditional or temporary immigration statuses are denied. Instead, they are offered a key that only allows entry into limited spaces—spaces to which the gatekeeper on the other side may deny access.

It is necessary to distinguish between eligibility and access. For example, a **Refugee Claimant (cf.)** has a document that shows they are eligible for health coverage from the federal government, but they are often denied access by health-care providers who choose to not accept this type of coverage, or are unaware of its existence. A refugee claimant in Nova Scotia, for example, is eligible to apply for provincial income assistance, but they might be denied access due to an agent who confuses them with sponsored refugees **(cf. Sponsorship)** and incorrectly turns them away as ineligible. A refugee claimant with a work permit (i.e. permission to work in Canada that is issued from Immigration, Refugees and Citizenship Canada [IRCC]) has a social insurance number (SIN) that makes them eligible for employment, but the employer might refuse access and deny applications based on discrimination. A refugee claimant who has received a positive decision on their refugee claim is eligible for provincial health coverage in Nova Scotia once they have applied for permanent residence; however, they might find themselves turned away by an agent who works for the provincial health insurance agency, the Medical Services Insurance agency (commonly referred to as MSI), but who is not familiar with the policy and simply says no. A refugee claimant might be denied access at a food bank because they don't have a health card, when this is not even an eligibility requirement! This list is endless.

The barriers listed in here are just a few examples of those that occur when front-line agents and institutional culture deny access *despite* eligibility. Refugee claimants in Nova Scotia and beyond also face lack of eligibility for essential services and benefits such as government-funded English-language training and settlement services, student loans; public housing, and the National Child Benefit (NCB).

A refugee claimant must apply separately for a work permit to be allowed to work in Canada. The processing times can be lengthy (sometimes months), resulting in the person being forced to apply for income assistance, rely on loans, or work "under the table" in sometimes unsafe or abusive work environments to make ends meet. This means refugee claimants are at a higher risk of poverty and of being taken advantage of by unscrupulous employers.

Compounding these challenges, interpreters are often not provided for refugee claimants accessing services. This is an accessibility issue. Service-providers bear the responsibility of providing accessible services to their clients. Passing this responsibility onto their clients is appalling, yet we do see refugee claimants who have low-level English or no English asked to provide their own interpreter in a meeting—sometimes resulting in children being used as interpreters, or there being no interpreter at all.

To list all the barriers refugee claimants face would require an entire book—and a long, exhausting, and shocking read it would be. The systemic and systematic barriers that refugee claimants face are numerous and intersecting, and do harm. People in Nova Scotia making refugee claims are a minority, and their status is widely misunderstood. Due to the smaller numbers in our province, the "culture of no" is likely more pervasive than in larger cities, and the policy pieces regarding refugee claimants are less developed, non-existent, or even factually incorrect.

Refugee claimants often find themselves forced to live on the margins of society—on the other side of the door—and are often thwarted from reaching their potential, prevented from contributing their skills, and, forced to live in uncertainty, unable to develop roots. The barriers are both intentional and unintentional—not to mention wildly inconsistent—and refugee claimants often require advocates to access services for which they are eligible. However, the picture is not entirely dark. The fact that we live in a country that has a process for refugee claimants to be heard is an essential foundation. Refugee claimants advocating **(cf. Activism & Advocacy)** for themselves and with service providers across the country are working to overcome barriers, change policy, and open doors. There are organizations that exist to support, provide services to, and advocate with refugee claimants **(cf. Settlement Services)**; however, such organizations are often underfunded, overworked, and reliant on private donations.

# boat peo·ple

## Shiva Nourpanah

Crossing large bodies of water is an inevitable part of the flight for many refugees seeking haven from their war-torn countries. Often travelling without documentation, refugees make ad hoc, dangerous arrangements in order to cross seas with the help of smugglers, and the risk of death by drowning, fatigue, or suffocation is very real. It is convenient to lay the blame for these deaths at the door of smugglers, with a fair amount of victim-blaming towards refugees themselves. However, the governments of destination countries who criminalize the act of seeking refuge and make the route towards safety increasingly onerous bear a fair portion of the responsibility. Furthermore, many of the states dedicated to patrolling their coasts and seas, ensuring as few refugees as possible make it through, are the same states that have exacerbated the conditions of insecurity and fragility in these people's home countries, creating the preconditions for flight and asylum.

Reliable statistics on those who die in the attempt to seek refuge on the high seas do not exist, with numbers fluctuating based on the season, weather, and **Countries of Origin (cf.)**. Despite the risks, many are prepared to undertake the journey, and indeed many do cross successfully. Nevertheless, images of soaking and exhausted women, children, and men, struggling or being rescued from their unseaworthy vessels, tossed up against the coastlines of Europe, North America, and Australia, appear regularly in mainstream media. These images perpetuate simplistic and racialized narratives about "Third World" countries stuck in perpetual cycles of violence, instability, and war, persecuting their own residents. Meanwhile, power-mongering between governments upon the global stage, deep global inequalities, and post-colonial histories—which are all too often the cause of war and violence leading to refugee exoduses—are generally overlooked as related issues in mainstream media.

The arrival of "boat people" has often propelled refugee affairs into national and global spotlights, sparking outcry, activism, and policy changes that may have lasting consequences. Some such significant moments in Canadian history are as follows.

• In 1986, 155 Tamils were left stranded in lifeboats off the shores of Newfoundland, and after floating for three days with little food and water, were rescued by the coast guard vessel *Leonard J. Crowley*.

• The arrival of the *Amelie* in 1987 off the coast of Shelburne, Nova Scotia, which was carrying 174 Sikhs, led indirectly to the establishment of the Halifax Refugee Clinic.

• In 2010, the MV *Sun Sea* arrived off the west coast of Canada carrying 492 people, ten months after the MV *Ocean Lady* brought in 76 people. All passengers stated they were Sri Lankans fleeing the civil war in their country. These arrivals were greeted with intense public and media interest. The refugee claimants were subjected to prolonged **Detention (cf.)** and "intensive interrogation" by government officials.[11] Their arrival fuelled the impetus to change the immigration legislation of the time, expanding the power of the government to detain arrivals and deny them of their rights, while launching new initiatives to patrol the Pacific coast and intercept "boat people" before they landed.

---

[11]Canadian Council for Refugees, media release, "Sun Sea: Five Years later," August 2015, http://ccrweb.ca/sites/ccrweb.ca/files/sun-sea-five-years-later.pdf.

# B

bo·gus
ref·u·gees

## Catherine Baillie Abidi

The "bogus refugee" is a socially constructed concept that has evolved over several decades and serves to disrupt the link between refugees and protection **(cf. Credibility)**. The accusation of "bogus" questions the basis of refugee rights—that of international protection from persecution—by implying that a **Refugee Claimant (cf.)** is not in genuine need of protection but instead is a fraudulent, dishonest person. The bogus refugee is a highly politicized concept that has been reinforced by many Canadian parliamentarians in order to maintain restrictive regulations built on exclusionary and xenophobic **(cf. Racism)** foundations. "Bogus" is a harmful label that calls into question the legitimacy of a claimant's need for protection, thus jeopardizing their safety from **Persecution (cf.)**.

cit·i·zen·ship

# Pauline Gardiner Barber

Whether or not we think much about it, citizenship is a fundamental aspect of all our lives—but most especially for asylum seekers and refugees. At its most general level, citizenship refers to legal membership in modern nation-states. Citizens are also defined by the existence of non-citizens, such as refugees. The main point to grasp about citizenship is that it designates people as either outsiders (foreigners) or insiders (citizens). Refugees attract public attention not solely because they are in need of protection, but also because they are uninvited outsiders who nonetheless are supposed to be accommodated and treated compassionately in accordance with the **1951 Refugee Convention & the Protocol of 1967 (cf.)**.

Scholars have noted two main distinctions between citizenship regimes. There are nations founded upon ethnic conceptions of nationhood, wherein membership is restrictive and based on descent and the ties of blood and lineage, are known as *jus sanguinis*, or "rule of blood." In such nations, even established resident minorities may be denied state membership and citizenship. One current example is that of the Rohingya people in Myanmar. The Rohingya are a stateless population of around 1 million persons who have long-standing residency but no citizenship rights in their country of residence. As recently as 2018, they continued to experience state-sponsored persecution, causing many to flee across the border into Bangladesh as refugees. Other contemporary examples of ethno-nationalism and *jus sanguinis* citizenship in action are Greece and Japan, both of which are marked by their reluctance to extend full membership rights, as citizens, to resident immigrant populations.

Alternatively, societies where civic conceptions of nationhood prevail are known as *jus soli*, or "rule of the soil," and are considered more accepting of immigrants as potential citizens. Historic settler societies that depended upon immigration, and still do today, such as the United States, Australia, New Zealand, and Canada, are examples of civic rather than ethnic polities. Citizenship scholars pay much attention to how such immigration nations, often under the rubric of multiculturalism, seek to create a sense of membership and belonging among their diverse immigrant populations. But here again, membership rights of certain groups can be contracted, as we see in the example of Donald Trump's Republican government in the US. Trump's anti-immigrant rhetoric during the 2018 mid-term elections included discussion of limiting birthright citizenship (status conferred through being born on US soil), which represents a troublesome recent example of the potential contraction of citizenship rights for certain long-term resident populations.

Theoretically, citizenship (by descent or residency) confers a legal identity and provides individuals with a set of rights and legal protections that include civil rights (such as personal liberties, freedom of expression, religious beliefs, and so on), social rights (for example, access to social services and such), and political rights (pertaining to the right to vote and run for office). Some theorists see these rights as having expanded over the last centuries and shifting, as a result of social struggles, from the exclusive domain of white, property-holding males to include working classes, women, and racialized minorities. But citizenship also confers on citizens a set of obligations and responsibilities that can expand and contract in accord with state policies and the legal system. The rights associated with citizenship can be awarded and taken away, perhaps best illustrated today by present political struggles over religious freedoms and women's reproductive rights.

Citizenship as a concept also has a subjective side and is closely tied to ideas (and ideals) of nationality and belonging to a particular polity. This takes us into the highly subjective realm of values and national ideologies. For example, Canadian political discourse espouses multiculturalism as a positive feature of Canadian life, yet immigration policies since the mid-twentieth century betray a tension between the balancing of economic and demographic purpose. The vast nation needs more people, but we privilege those who are youthful and are considered to have high levels of economic and human capital (such as particular job skills and educational credentials) rather than those seeking a better, safer life.

A reverse logic applies to asylum seekers and refugees when those defined as economic migrants are disqualified as legitimate refugees. Similarly, with refugee policy, the humanitarian component of Canadian policy (and ideological claims about Canada as a caring and compassionate nation) is frequently muddied by arguments about how refugees can benefit the economy. We can see these tensions reflected globally, in political debates and divides over immigration and refugee policy; how many immigrants, including refugees, are acceptable, and why, or why not? In many countries such debates cast immigrants and refugees as competing with citizens for jobs and entitlements to social rights—this despite the large body of research that challenges such negative assumptions.

# coun·try of or·i·gin

## Shiva Nourpanah

Sometimes referred to as "sending" or "source countries," the term, in relation to refugees, refers to the countries where conditions of instability, violence, and insecurity lead to the flight of its people. Refugee flows from these countries may be large or small, or they may fluctuate from year to year. General information about the situation in countries of origin, in particular about the groups facing persecution, helps authorities to make informed decisions on refugee claims. However, given the difficulty of gathering reliable information in conditions of instability and insecurity, country-of-origin information by itself may not always be a good indicator of the validity of individual refugee claims.

By June 2018, according to the **United Nations High Commissioner for Refugees (cf. UNHCR)**, there were an estimated 6.3 million Syrian refugees.[12] Afghanistan, the source country with the second-highest number of refugees, numbered

---

[12] Syria is presently the top source country for refugees at the date of this book's publication.

2.6 million refugees. South Sudan was the third largest source country for refugees at 2.4 million.[13] Before Syria dislodged Afghanistan as the source country with the world's highest population of refugees in 2015, Afghan refugees had been the largest refugee group for many years—not surprising considering Afghanistan has been the site of both civil and foreign warring factions since the USSR's invasion of 1978–79.

Other top "sending countries" in recent years are Somalia, Sudan, Democratic Republic of Congo, Iraq, and Myanmar. Many of these countries are on Canada's "moratoria" list[14] of countries, meaning that refugee claimants from these countries are not returned to their country of origin even if their individual refugee claim is not accepted. This is a controversial practice, since although it is preferable to **Deportation (cf.)**, it means that claimants may face a long time—often many years—in legal limbo.[15]

The continuity of war and generalized insecurity is not a necessary condition for producing refugees. Countries with stable governments have proved themselves capable of virulent persecution of minorities and particular social groups: refugees have escaped persecution by fleeing from Chinese and Iranian authorities for many decades, and Hungary's treatment of its Roma population has provoked international outrage.

---

[13] Figures at a Glance," website for the UNHCR, last modified June 19, 2018, https://www.unhcr.org/figures-at-a-glance.html.

[14] "Moratoria" countries are those that the Government of Canada recognizes are unsafe, and thus will not deport refugees whose claim has failed back to them.

[15] Canadian Council for Refugees, media release, "Lives on Hold: Nationals of Moratoria Countries Living in Limbo," July 2005, https://ccrweb.ca/sites/ccrweb.ca/files/livesonhold.pdf.

No matter their country of origin, refugees deserve a fair hearing and evaluation of their claim. Denying or limiting refugee claims solely based on their country of origin goes against the spirit of the 1951 Refugee Convention. Such restrictions, known as "designated countries of origin" policies in the Canadian context, curtail the international rights of refugees in the interest of bureaucratic efficiency.

# C

cred·i·bil·i·ty

## Josh Judah & Sara Mahaney

Under the *Note on Burden and Standard of Proof in Refugee Claims* [16] , from the United Nations High Commissioner for Refugees, it is stated:

"[c]redibility is established where the applicant has presented a claim which is coherent and plausible, not contradicting generally known facts, and therefore is, on balance, capable of being believed."

Credibility issues can arise in a number of different ways. For example, when there are inconsistencies or discrepancies within the **Refugee Claimant's (cf.)** testimony or between the claimant's testimony and the documentation filed, or when a claimant fails to be specific about the events upon which their claim is based, or fails to provide independent corroborating evidence of the basis for their claim.

According to the Note on Burden and Standard of Proof: "There is no necessity for the applicant to prove all facts to such a standard

---

[16] UNHCR, *Note on Burden and Standard of Proof in Refugee Claims,* (December 16, 1998), http://www.refworld.org/docid/3ae6b3338.html.

that the adjudicator is fully convinced that all factual assertions are true." In cases where there is an "element of doubt in the mind of the adjudicator," the applicant should be given the "benefit of the doubt" and "any element of doubt should not prejudice the applicant's claim."

Credibility is sometimes confused with honesty. Credibility and truthfulness are not the same things. There are many examples of claimants who cannot provide credible testimony in regard to some details of their claim. For example, an individual who is tortured may not be able to accurately describe the building in which the incident occurred, but it would not, however, be reasonable to conclude that the claimant is lying.

In some cases, it is not feasible that a claimant would have specific corroborating documentary evidence of their claim. Any lack of corroborating documentary evidence must be considered by the Immigration and Refugee board member in the context of the claim. The *Note on Burden and Standard of Proof* recognizes that an adjudicator "will often need to depend entirely on the oral statements of the applicant and make an assessment in light of the objective situation in the country of origin."

Sometimes the evidence a claimant is able to put forward is from family members or may for some other reason be perceived to be "self-serving." However, even in such cases, that evidence must be given its due weight by the board member.

There are Immigration and Refugee Board "Chairperson guidelines"[17] that recognize that certain claimants can have

---

[17] For full list of guidelines please refer to https://irb-cisr.gc.ca/en/legal-policy/policies/Pages/chairperson-guideline.aspx.

particular difficulty establishing that their claims are credible. For example, Guideline 4[18] for women refugee claimants fearing gender-related persecution and Guideline 9[19] for claims involving sexual orientation and gender identity and expression set out various considerations for evaluating the credibility of such a claimant's evidence.

---

[18] "Chairperson Guidelines 4: Women Refugee Claimants Fearing Gender-Related Persecution," website for Immigration and Refugee Board of Canada, last modified July 6, 2018, https://irb-cisr.gc.ca/en/legal-policy/policies/Pages/GuideDir04.aspx.

[19] Immigration and Refugee Board of Canada (website); the "Chairperson Guideline 9: Proceedings Before the IRB Involving Sexual Orientation and Gender Identity and Expression" page; https://irb-cisr.gc.ca/en/legal-policy/policies/Pages/GuideDir09.aspx.

# de·por·ta·tion

## Julie Chamagne

The refugee determination process, which differs from jurisdiction to jurisdiction, flows from this basic principle that people in need of protection will not be deported.

Deportation, in Canadian law, is present at the first and last stages of a refugee claim **(cf. Refugee Claimant)**. When someone makes a claim for protection and they are deemed inadmissible to Canada, they are immediately issued a removal order. This order will become a deportation order if they are not successful in their claim, in subsequent appeals, or other remedies. It is not insignificant that the entire refugee determination procedure is carried out with this removal order hanging above a person's head. Their conditional status and this relentless threat of deportation mean that refugee claimants must live under the constant fear of a negative decision, which underscores and contributes to their marginalization in society.

Canada has no process for keeping track of what happens when failed refugee claimants are returned to their **Country of Origin (cf.)**, although there have been several occasions where people have been killed or subjected to more **Persecution (cf.)** and ill-treatment when they were returned after deportation.

Non-status migrants who do not fit the refugee definition and who cannot regularize their status through other means are also subject to deportation. Deportation is not always immediate and may occur many years—even decades—after a person's first entry to Canada. As long as someone does not acquire Canadian citizenship, there are instances where a person could lose their status and be subject to deportation.

# de·ten·tion

## Julie Chamagne

It may come as a surprise that Canada detains children, people with mental health issues, and vulnerable people who have suffered trauma and **Persecution (cf.)**. In certain circumstances, when asylum seekers arrive without papers and are intercepted by the Canada Border Services Agency (CBSA), they are placed in prison. In Halifax, they are detained in the Central Nova Scotia Correctional Facility (also known as Burnside Jail) alongside convicted prisoners, while in other, more populated places, such as Toronto, they are kept in immigration detention centres designed for their specific situation.

Detention re-traumatizes and re-victimizes people who have already been persecuted, not to mention it deprives them of their liberty and dignity. In addition to the detrimental psychological effects of detention, **Refugee Claimants (cf.)** must also tell their stories in these conditions—under extreme stress and pressure, with little access to interpreters, counsel, and others who can help confirm and gather information—which can have a negative effect on the outcome of their claims for protection, and ultimately lead to deportation.

Refugees often feel betrayed, shocked, and humiliated when they arrive in Canada—their country of refuge, a place they have heard of their whole lives as being a bastion of human rights **(cf. Human & Refugee Rights)**, of acceptance, and tolerance—only to be thrown in jail.

Last year a young man from Afghanistan arrived in a container ship after having fled the Taliban in his country. He was detained for several months and had this to say after his release:

> *When I come in Canada at first I am go hospital and after they put me in the jail and my health is not good and jail for two month it's like two years and every time I am not sleeping good because I scare it's jail and I am refugee it's for me hard my mind my face and my health day by day it's gone bad and the first time I see like that place in my life.*
>
> *We are coming in Canada to save our life we need happy life like you people we need help from you people and love.*
>
> *–Ali Reza Mohammed* [20]

---

[20] Quoted, with permission, from personal communication with contributor.

# dis·place·ment

D

## Shiva Nourpanah

The term "displacement" is used to describe situations where groups of people are moved from their homelands due to external factors outside of their control, thereby losing their livelihoods and traditions. Although refugees are by definition displaced, not every displacement can be described as a refugee movement. Displacement does not have to involve fear of persecution or targeted oppression; rather, it is more usually associated with development projects and environmental and climate changes. Although displacement may result in international border crossings, it is more common within the borders of nation-states. Therefore, displacement is sometimes mistakenly viewed as an internal problem rather than an international issue.

However, **UNHCR (cf.)** has recognized internally displaced people **(cf. Internal Displacement)** as falling within the scope of its mandate, acknowledging that flight and forced movements may not always propel people over international borders. In fact, given the difficulty of accessing these groups in order to deliver relief and assistance, UNHCR considers them among the most vulnerable populations in the world.

Displacement often targets the vulnerable and marginalized members of society. Homeless people, nomads, slum-dwellers, indigenous populations, ghetto communities—such populations are all too commonly viewed as superfluous and therefore disposable in relation to large projects, whether run by the state or private companies. Such projects—ranging from dams in India to the Olympic games in British Columbia—often become involved in unethical and controversial displacement practices, though some scholars argue that it is possible to carry out such projects and the associated movements in respectful, responsible ways, for instance by ensuring that their benefits are worth the cost to human lives by being distributed in equitable and fair ways— rather than vanishing as the profit of a privileged few.

## ec·o·nom·ic mi·grant

# Marianela Fuertes

The difference between an economic **Migrant (cf.)** and a **Refugee (cf.)**, under international law, stems from the factors that compel the person to leave their **Country of Origin (cf.)**. For the international human rights system **(cf. Human & Refugee Rights)**, it is crucial to distinguish between people who are actively forced out of their country against their will (refugees) and those who could stay but prefer to immigrate (economic migrants). The distinction between economic migrants and refugees as per the **1951 Refugee Convention (cf.)**, then, is based on the threat to personal integrity.

A person who decides to leave their own country for economic reasons exercises the freedom to compare the cost of staying in their country versus the cost of immigrating. (It is important to mention that the decision to leave might well be made under other pressures, but nonetheless there is the ability to exercise some level of autonomy.) Meanwhile the protection that the international community is bound to provide to refugees is linked to compelling circumstances where the person is not able to voluntarily decide whether to leave their country.

Countries recognize this difference and have procedures to immigrate under the economic category that play an important part in their national immigration policies, attracting the type of workers, investors, and professionals required by the country's economic priorities.

# en·vi·ron·men·tal ref·u·gees

E

## Shiva Nourpanah

Imagine living by a shoreline and watching the sea rise due to factors completely beyond your control, knowing that the waves will swallow up your home in the next few years. This is predicted to happen to 8 million Pacific Islanders by 2050. Some estimates put the total number of environmental refugees, worldwide, at around 200 million by that time.

Environmental or climate refugees are people who have lost or are in danger of losing their homes due to environmental and climate-change factors. Rising sea levels is just one phenomenon leading to forced displacement. Environmental degradation leading to loss of livelihoods is another, and it is even harder to measure. It seems that nobody wants to bear the responsibility for dealing with the consequences of these global changes.

Environmentally-caused flights are marked by the absence of state persecution **(cf. Persecution)** coupled with the failure of state protection **(cf. Statelessness & State Protection)**. Usually no other viable alternatives to flight from traditional homelands seem available. In most cases, the line between human-induced and natural disasters is quite thin—after all, what is natural? The consequences of many natural disasters are exacerbated by long-term human activity, not least the long-standing neglect of ethnic minorities or marginalized social groups by government services, leaving them in particularly vulnerable positions when disaster strikes. Conversely, many natural disasters come about as a result of human activity. Unregulated development focused only on profit for a privileged few may lead to scenarios involving unwanted **Displacement (cf.)**.

**UNHCR (cf.)** and the **1951 Refugee Convention (cf.)** do not offer protection to environmental refugees. Indeed, the international protection framework around such displacements is quite thin. It may be time to expand the scope of international protection to offer clear, comprehensive solutions to these refugees whose numbers are set to dramatically increase.

# fam·i·ly re·u·ni·fi·ca·tion

## Katie Tinker

Many **Refugees (cf.)** and **Refugee Claimants (cf.)** who come to Canada have reluctantly had to leave family members behind in order to get here. There are many reasons why this happens. It may be because there was only enough money for one family member to make the journey, or because the journey itself was considered too risky for more vulnerable members of the family. Perhaps it was impossible to obtain visas for all family members. Or perhaps there was a member of the family who was detained **(cf. Detention)** or unable to be located at the time of travel. Whatever the circumstances, once a refugee becomes settled in Canada, and once their **Status** is secured **(cf.)**, reuniting with overseas family members—some of whom may be living in dangerous or precarious situations—is often urgent and high priority.

There are different options for refugees to bring their family members to Canada, depending on the channel through which they themselves arrived, and how their family members are related to them. Refugees who have been resettled in Canada through government or private sponsorship **(cf. Resettlement)** may submit what is known as a One-year Window of Opportunity provision

(OYW) application to bring dependent family members (spouses and children under the age of twenty-two) to Canada, as long as those family members were listed on the resettled individual's immigration forms, and as long the application is submitted within one year of their arrival in Canada. Those who apply for asylum inside Canada may apply for **Permanent Residence (cf.)** once their asylum case receives approval, and may include dependent family members in their permanent residence applications. In these cases, overseas dependents are allowed to travel to Canada once the principal applicant is officially landed, and once they are deemed to have met all the eligibility requirements to become permanent residents.

Options are limited for those who wish to help non-dependent family members come to Canada. There is a visa program for sponsoring parents and grandparents, but the number of spaces offered through this program is limited, and vastly insufficient to meet the present demand. Other family members may be assisted through one of Canada's refugee sponsorship programs— if their relative in Canada has access to sufficient resources and sponsorship partners—or they may qualify to immigrate independently through one of Canada's economic immigration streams.

Without exception, every available avenue for family reunification involves significant processing times—often years—and these delays can be agonizing for the families involved **(cf. Limbo)**. Parents find it difficult to understand why they must miss years of their children's lives simply because of a sluggish bureaucracy. Marriages sometimes fall apart under the strain of prolonged separation.

One young woman, who asked to remain anonymous, spoke about her experience waiting to join her father, whose in-Canada refugee claim was accepted in 2011. The Canadian visa office in her country is one of the slowest in the world, and so it was six years before she, her mother, and her younger brother were able to join her father in Canada. Unfortunately, only months prior to their arrival, her father was diagnosed with a terminal brain tumour, making those years of separation particularly heartbreaking. "Canada is a very good country," she says, "but the waiting times are too long. My brother was nine, and I was fourteen, when my father left. When I came here, I didn't even remember his face."[21]

---

[21] Quoted from personal communication with contributor.

# F

forced
mi·gra·tion

## Amara Bangura

According to **UNHCR (cf.)**, presently 68.5 million people are forcibly displaced worldwide, including 40 million internally displaced **(cf. Internal Displacement)**, 25.4 million **Refugees (cf.)**, and 3.1 million **Asylum Seekers (cf.)**[22] . The number of people forced to flee their homes continues to rise, and we are now witnessing record highs—in fact, 44,400 people are forced to flee their homes each day due to conflict and persecution.[23]

The armed struggle in Liberia in the 1990s led to the collapse of what was already an embattled economy. The conflict almost completely destroyed the physical infrastructure that was built more than a century ago, and more than half of the country's population was maimed, killed, or displaced **(cf. Displacement)**. Many of the civilian victims fled to neighbouring Sierra Leone, a country most had never visited. The living conditions for refugees in Sierra Leone were tough. They suffered from a lack of basic amenities including proper shelter, food, health-care support, and economic opportunities.

---

[22] "Figures at a Glance," UNHCR website.
[23] See note 22 above.

Two years later, with support from Liberian warlord Charles Taylor, the Revolutionary United Front rebels (RUF), led by a former army corporal, Foday Saybanah Sankoh, launched his invasion into Sierra Leone. By any measure, the Sierra Leone Civil War was atrocious. The rebels used rape, amputation, abduction, looting, and forced labour as common tactics to ruin what was already a country suffering from many years of political misrule. Civilians were the primary targets. Accurate statistics of the atrocities are impossible to obtain, but the United Nations Development Program (2006), reported the estimated death toll from the decade-long civil war to be seventy thousand, and roughly 2.6 million people were displaced from their homes.[24] The Liberian refugees, who had sought safety in Sierra Leone, became refugees for the second time during the Sierra Leone invasion.

After eleven years of vicious fighting, a peace deal was signed in Lomé in 2002, which eventually brought the brutal civil war to an end. The impacts of the conflict and forced migration were significant, particularly for those separated from their families. Those forced to flee have to live with deep psychological wounds, which make returning **"Home" (cf.)** difficult; their original home country becomes a reminder of the tragic experience that made them refugees to begin with—so much so that many prefer to remain refugees for life.

For those who wish to return, the policies of host countries and the resulting social challenges do not favour them. Refugees who return home often face new challenges as they attempt to rebuild

---

[24] UN Development Program, case study, "Sierra Leone: Evaluation of UNDP Assistance to Conflict-Affected Countries," 2006, http://web. undp.org/evaluation/documents/thematic/conflict/SierraLeone. pdf.

their lives where basic life amenities are either scarce or non-existent.

Returning home **(cf. Repatriation)** takes time and is fraught with challenges. Most returnees experience trauma and stigmatization when they return, and as a result of such challenges and limited opportunities, many may choose to look for the opportunity to migrate again.

# gen·der

# G

## Evangelia Tastsoglou

By contrast to biological sex, gender refers to the socially constructed notions of masculinity and femininity—i.e. to the masculine and feminine roles and their associated expectations and practices, as well as the institutions reinforcing them and the identities built thereon. Scientific research acknowledges that biological sex is not binary but exists on a continuum, and that gender identities do not necessarily coincide with biological sex, as in the case of transgender individuals.

Gender plays a major role in every step of the migration process, from making the decision to leave and planning for departure, to modalities of travel, risks along the way **(cf. Journey)**, and settlement and integration opportunities, practices, and outcomes **(cf. Settlement Services)**. During **Forced Migration (cf.)**, women experience higher levels of vulnerability to sexual and gender-based violence than men and higher mortality rates at borders and dangerous crossings.

As a form of social division, gender is intersectional in that it operates in conjunction with other social divisions such as social class, race, ethnicity, religion, age, sexual orientation, and ability, to produce unique social positions, identities, strengths, and vulnerabilities for different categories of people.

## gov·ern·ment as·sis·ted ref·u·gees (GARs)

# Benjamin Amaya

The **United Nations High Commissioner for Refugees (UNHCR) (cf.)**, in collaboration with private sponsors, identifies refugees for **Resettlement (cf.)** in Canada and refers them to the Canadian government.

Refugees comprise about 15% of the permanent residents **(cf. Permanent Residence)** admitted to Canada each year. Approximately 50% of refugees in Canada are government-assisted (also known as government-sponsored). In 2015, 9,488 refugees were given permanent resident **Status (cf.)** in Canada; 9,748 arrived as privately sponsored refugees and 811 as members of the Blended Visa Office-Referred Category.

The Resettlement Assistance Program (RAP), under the authority of the Department of Immigration, Refugees and Citizenship Canada (IRCC) helps GARs whose initial resettlement in Canada is entirely supported by the Government of Canada or Quebec. A number of responsibilities and tasks related to resettlement are shared with provincial governments as well as non-governmental organizations (NGOs). Through the RAP, the Canadian government subsidizes refugees' transportation to Canada as well as their initial living expenses, such as food and accommodation, for a maximum period of one year; it also provides them with help in finding employment and language training once they arrive.

# grat·i·tude

**G**

## Katie Tinker

Gratitude is an idea that is often linked with refugee narratives. In some ways, this is inevitable. People who leave their countries of **Citizenship (cf.)** out of fear for their lives must find another country that will take them in. Those who find their way to places like Canada, where they are afforded the chance to resettle **(cf. Resettlement)**, apply for citizenship, and build new lives, may naturally feel lucky—especially when they compare themselves to other refugees who have ended up in host countries where they do not enjoy such opportunities, or to their fellow citizens who were unable to leave at all.

In the years following the Canadian government's 2015 announcement that it would significantly increase the numbers of refugees, primarily Syrian, who would be resettled in Canada, stories began to appear regularly in the Canadian media profiling some of the new arrivals and reporting on their experiences as they adjusted to their new **Home (cf.).** The theme of many of these stories was how thankful the refugees were for the welcome they had received in Canada. [25]

---

[25] *CBC News*, "Syrian Refugee Family in Toronto Grateful for Canadian

Of course, those who have experienced **Persecution (cf.)** and forced **Displacement (cf. also Forced Migration)** have every right to speak about their experience, and gratitude may well be one of the principle emotions defining the resettlement chapter of their story. Furthermore, for Canadians who supported the government's efforts to expand Canada's refugee resettlement program, hearing expressions of gratitude from those who have benefitted may feel like a welcome affirmation of their moral instincts. These outcomes are not necessarily negative.

However, some have noted that an excessive focus on this type of gratitude narrative in public discourse may be problematic. For one thing, it places refugees in the role of victim, ignoring or devaluing the fact that they may have taken great risks and overcome tremendous hurdles in an effort to get themselves and their family members to safety. Meanwhile, those in the host country, many of whom have made little or no individual sacrifice, are encouraged to see themselves as saviours for no reason other than having been lucky enough to be born into safety and affluence.

Beyond this, stories of gratitude may engender warm feelings, but they may also be masking the whole truth. For people who have

Welcome," June 16, 2016, https://www.cbc.ca/amp/1.3516773; Patrick White, "Syrian Refugee Family Thankful for Freedom in Canada," *The Globe and Mail*, October 9, 2016, https://www.theglobeandmail. com/news/national/three-years-after-leaving-syria-family-grateful-for-freedom-in-canada/article32312834/; Tracy Nagai, "Syrian Refugees Show Gratitude as One Year Anniversary Fast Approaches," *Global News*, October 10, 2016, https://globalnews.ca/news/2994238/ syrian-refugees-show-gratitude-as-one-year-anniversary-fast-approaches/.

had to leave their homes, whose lives have been upended, and who may have lost loved ones, their gratitude having been offered a chance at a new life may lie alongside other emotions, such as grief for what they have lost, trauma, or stress caused by the challenges of adapting to a new culture.

As Shree Paradkar argues in her *Toronto Star* column: "While many refugees are grateful to be here, that same gratitude can become a chokehold when it is the only acceptable emotion 'allowed.'"[26] Dina Nayeri writes eloquently about what this restrictiveness was like for her as a young Iranian refugee living in the US: "[...] they wanted our salvation story as a talisman, no more. No one ever asked what our house in Iran looked like, what fruits we grew in our yard, what books we read, what music we loved and what it felt like now not to understand any of the songs on the radio. No one asked if we missed our cousins or grandparents or best friends."[27]

Creating a space in which refugees are encouraged to speak openly about all aspects of their experience is important. For refugees themselves, it not only offers a way of moving beyond the more difficult parts of their story, but also may help them feel more connected to those around them in their new home. For

---

[26] Shree Paradkar, "Expecting Gratitude from Refugees Is About Bolstering Our Own Saviour Complex," *The Star* (Toronto), July 4, 2018, https://www.thestar.com/opinion/star-columnists/2018/07/04/expecting-gratitude-from-refugees-is-about-bolstering-our-own-saviour-complex.html.

[27] Dina Nayari, "The Ungrateful Refugee: 'We have no debt to repay'," *The Guardian*, April 4, 2017, https://www.theguardian.com/world/2017/apr/04/dina-nayeri-ungrateful-refugee.

the host society, exposing ourselves to truthful narratives is a vital way of learning about the world and of transcending the inherent ignorance of our privilege. It is to our great disadvantage when we ignore these stories and focus only on the gratitude we expect or demand.

## health & health·care

# Wenche Gausdal

Refugees need a holistic and culturally safe approach to their health-care needs in order to settle successfully in Canada. Since the introduction of the Immigration and Refugee Protection Act (IRPA, 2002) **(cf. Legislation)**, Canada's selection of refugees **(cf. GARs)** is focused on those who need the most protection, that is, those who are more likely to have experienced violence and lived with limited access to food, shelter, health care, and safety. Consequently, many refugees have health or disability issues that require attention.

The Nova Scotia Department of Health and Wellness and the Nova Scotia Health Authority have invested in cultural competency policies, training, and resources in primary care and hospital settings, including the creation of the Newcomer Health Clinic (the primary care clinic for refugees) in 2015. Despite these efforts, refugees still face systemic barriers. Health-care providers require education regarding refugee health issues. Interpretation must be available for services such as specialists, dentists, optometrists, and services for people with disabilities.

Reluctance of health-care providers to become Interim Federal Health Program (IFHP) providers must be addressed.[28]


# Gillian Smith

Research and interest into the social determinants of health (SDH) are abundant in Canada, yet a key SDH is often missing from the list: immigration status **(cf. Status)**. Access to health care is inextricably linked to immigration status, so immigration status must be viewed and explored as an SDH. **Refugee Claimant Status (cf.)** has a profound negative impact on many aspects of their lives, including their access to health care.

It is not uncommon for people in Canada with access to the universal health-care system to assume it is available for all those residing in Canada. We pride ourselves on this perceived achievement, and in theory it appears that we are meeting the health-care needs of some of the most vulnerable. Since refugee claimants are not eligible for provincial health coverage until they have had their refugee **Hearing (cf.)** and been deemed protected persons, the federal government provides health coverage under the Interim Federal Health Program (IFHP). In theory, the IFHP is excellent: a robust program providing coverage for basic, urgent, and even supplemental care, but in practice, it is rife with administrative complications that create barriers to health care for refugee claimants. In fact, the program has been the focal point of anti-refugee partisan politics.

---

[28] See next contributor's entry for more on the IFHP.

Due to the issues surrounding the IFHP, access to health care through this program is often dependent on advocacy **(cf. Activism & Advocacy)**. Macro-level advocacy campaigns to push the federal government to restore the program after devastating cuts in June 2012 were successful after years of collaborative activism across Canada that took the issue all the way to the Federal Court. Since April 2016, eligibility for comprehensive care under the IFHP has been reinstated for refugee claimants; however, most of the administrative **Barriers (cf.)** that prevented access prior to the cuts remain an issue. The coverage was taken away by one federal government and restored by the next, but refugee claimants still face lack of access. Micro- and meso-level advocacy are continually necessary to turn IFHP eligibility into concrete access to health-care services in the community.

As an example, the Newcomer Health Clinic (NHC) in Halifax, which serves refugees and refugee claimants, was born out of advocacy. It began in early 2014 as an informal, volunteer-based, ad hoc response to cuts to the IFHP and a lack of family doctors in Halifax accepting refugees as patients. It took one physician willing to volunteer a day a week, in collaboration with the Immigrant Services Association of Nova Scotia (ISANS) and the Halifax Refugee Clinic to initiate what is now a formalized, culturally aware, preventative health and primary medical services clinic that is funded by the government of Nova Scotia.

There are so few family doctors accepting IFHP coverage outside of the Newcomer Health Clinic that most refugee claimants would not have access to primary health care if not for the Newcomer Health Clinic. Walk-in clinics in Halifax do not accept IFHP coverage, despite efforts to get them on board. Accessing health-care services limited to places that are supposed to accept IFHP coverage, such as hospitals, some pharmacies, some specialists, and particular dental offices, is a challenge due to the number of front-line staff who are unaware of how to process the coverage and so act as gatekeepers. It is also made difficult by other issues, such as pre-approval claims being rejected, slow payouts, and difficulty communicating with the IFHP administrator. Refugee claimants often get bills for health services that were supposed to be covered, and this can result in anxiety and reluctance to access care. Health-care providers accepting IFHP coverage and providing access with few barriers quickly become overwhelmed by the demand, and may stop accepting new patients as a result.

These many administrative and practical barriers make health-care providers reluctant to use IFHP, and make the process confusing for refugee claimants and refugees. These barriers add yet another layer of complexity to the myriad refugee health-care issues, such as language interpretation and cultural competence. Nevertheless, a refugee claimant's status makes them ineligible for a provincial health card and dependent on the IFHP, which requires ongoing advocacy to ensure their access to care—just like receiving a key to unlock a door, but having to convince the person on the other side to let you in.

# hear·ing

# Josh Judah & Sara Mahaney

The hearing is the opportunity for the **Refugee Claimant (cf.)** to present their testimony and evidence to the Immigration and Refugee Board (IRB) **(cf. Legislation)**. It is also the opportunity for the IRB board member assigned to the claim to assess the evidence and decide the case.

The legal hearing, in which the refugee claimant stands before a board member who decides the success or failure of their application for legal **Status (cf.)**, is incredibly high-stakes. The hearing is generally the claimant's only opportunity, after a long and arduous **Journey (cf.)**, to convince a single board member to grant them refugee protection.

In Atlantic Canada, more often than not hearings for refugee claimants are conducted via video conference, with the board member (and oftentimes an interpreter, if required) located in Montreal. Given the importance of these hearings, some may question the soundness of requiring a decision-maker to assess a claimant's claim, including their **Credibility (cf.)**, at such physical remove.

In the vast majority of legal proceedings, the party who has the onus to prove their case controls how their case is presented. A legal process under which a claimant can decide how their evidence is presented enables the claimant to present their claim more effectively. The claimant understands the breadth and nuance of their case. However, at refugee determination hearings, the board member deciding the claim for protection asks questions first, after which the claimant's counsel will have the opportunity to follow up with any clarification or other questions that may be required. As a result, the claimant's immediate ability to answer questions from the board member is key, and therefore it is important that the claimant prepare for this rather unique process in advance through mock hearings.

During questioning by the board member, the role of the claimant's counsel generally is not to object to the board member's questions but to protect the claimant's interest in a fair hearing, such as by being alert to whether the interpreter is adequately translating the claimant's evidence. The board member's questioning will generally be non-adversarial, focused instead on acquiring the evidence necessary to assess the merits of the claim. However, the board member's questions may become more pointed and confrontational if he or she has a concern about inconsistencies or other credibility issues **(cf. Credibility)**.

The hearing may run longer than the scheduled time. This usually results in the matter being adjourned to a new date for a hearing continuation. The delay between the first and second part of a hearing can be as little as a day and as much as two years.

After questioning is complete, the claimant's counsel will have the opportunity to present to the board member any submissions summarizing the supporting evidence that must be met in order for the board member to grant refugee protection to the claimant. In some cases these submissions are presented orally at the conclusion of the hearing. In other cases the submissions take written form and are filed within a few weeks of the conclusion of the hearing.

Even in the case of oral submissions at the end of a hearing, some cases are adjourned and the board member will issue a written decision that the claimant will later receive in the mail. In some cases, the board member will issue a positive decision granting the claim for refugee status at the end of the hearing, reading their reasons for the decision into the record. One of the most fulfilling experiences for legal counsel is witnessing a client's relief in receiving such a decision, watching as the claimant realizes that their claim has been accepted and seeing the weight lift from their heavily burdened shoulders.

# H home

## Yanery Navarro Vigil

*Note from the contributor: My intention in writing in the following tone was to discuss in an organic-feeling way concepts that, in their very origin, have a poetic undertone. Having lived what these concepts mean in my flesh, in a process of losing and regaining, making them again part of both my epistemic and my ontological field, I find it almost impossible to speak about them in "concrete terms." Once a concept dwells in your being, it is hard to speak "about them" and not "from them." Placing myself in the reader's shoes, I wanted to open up the concept in a way that allows their experience to sift into the room, as every text must allow for interpretation. As someone who has experienced homelessness, along with statelessness, I find it hard to express this experience linearly. Factual- and research-based are not exactly compatible with experience-based and/or first-voice. Or perhaps it is me who can only speak in these terms about "concepts" in which I deeply dwell and that so deeply dwell in me.*

**What is "home"?**

Home is not a physical place, even though the land, as a geographical space, may be part of it. Home is a depth that everyone carries within. A microcosm of being fed and fulfilled through a body. A body of connections. A being who is everyone. It is a progressive motion that constantly adds elements, pieces, contents into its own body. And it is this extended physical body that supports our lives.

There is no life without home. For home is a beginning, as simple as it is indispensable, and always framed inside an elastic *topos*; one which might encompass a country or a nation, but also the planet or the entire universe. It is at once atomizable and universalizable. For it is home that expands and contracts all human movement. Home is finding oneself in a moment of motionlessness which, paradoxically, cannot stop moving. It entails a primeval care and protection, a basic need to survive, to adapt, to be well—to well-being.

From womb to tomb, we keep building home. Home is where a person becomes their self; where the actions of settling and belonging are accomplished. Home sustains self and opens for others. Home is the body that connects the inside with the outside. It is a body of relations. Consequently, it is an embodied space, a refuge. A repository of meaning. A threshold where the external and the internal are birthed. As an act of the imagination, home carries our memory and memories until its final dissolution. Home is a network of references and representations, a collection of epistemic crops: that collective cultivation we call culture. Since humans originate as people, they also originate as culture. Home is our first migration to this life, a migration in which roots mix with movement in a chain of motion. Home is that chain of migrations that comprise us from conception, as a guest in another's body, to inception, as a guest in others' cultures.

We are all immigrants. Immigrants shaped and transformed in an invisible process of transculturation—a process that can only take place at home. Without a home, this invisible process is one of assimilation, in which one loses oneself in favour of a dominant other. Home is who each human is. Home is that other to which one comes back, every day, as oneself.

# hu·man & ref·u·gee rights

## Marianela Fuertes

When a person has been recognized as a refugee in accordance with Article 1A (2) of the **1951 Refugee Convention (cf.)** [29] , he/she has the right to be treated in some ways as a citizen of the state that provides the asylum. All the rights and freedoms that any foreigner who is a legal resident enjoys should be guaranteed to a refugee. This principle is founded in the recognition that all humans are equal and have the right to be treated equally before the law. These are also the principles that inspired the universal system of human rights that emerged after the Second World War, following the deep crisis that haunted the civilization that saw humanity submerged into the most horrendous violations of human rights. It is important to remember where we as humans come from and how far we still are from being a global community.

Eleanor Roosevelt perhaps put it best when she wrote the following words:

---

[29] UN General Assembly, *Convention Relating to the Status of Refugees*

*We must relearn the meaning of that noble word "respect," which is the only sound and enduring basis for any relationship among peoples, as it is among individuals. We must learn to respect the various methods of development of new nations so long as they grant to the individual certain basic rights. We cannot say to them: "If you will accept our way of life we will help you." If we are going to build a strong and peaceful world, we must be intelligent enough to help new nations in terms of their needs and not of our personal theories.[30]*

The most important rights to refugee protection are also the fundamental rights stated in the *Universal Declaration of Human Rights* and in most charters of rights and freedoms in the constitutions of liberal states.

The rights that should be guaranteed to refugees comprise more than physical safety. The person recognized as a refugee has basic civil, social, and economic rights. Every refugee should have access to medical care. Every adult should have the right to work, and all refugee children should have access to education **(cf. Youth & Second Generation)**. However, social and economic rights usually depend on the conditions of the economic possibilities of the state. Sometimes the state is unable to provide those benefits for their own native community. When the amount of refugees exceeds the capacity of the social and economic condition of the country, the government has to take measures that affect the assistance given to refugees. Usually this happens

---

[30] Eleanor Roosevelt, *Tomorrow Is Now: It Is Today that We Must Create the World of the Future* (New York: Penguin Classics; Reprint edition, 2012).

when a humanitarian crisis takes place and a neighbouring country suddenly has to receive hundreds of people. In addition, when a large-scale inflow of refugees occurs, then the asylum state may have to restrict certain fundamental rights, such as freedom of movement, freedom to work, or proper schooling for children. Those situations unveil the asylum country's lack of, or insufficient access to, the resources needed to face the crisis. In such cases it is necessary for them to work in conjunction with the international community. UNHCR provides assistance at such times to sustain those refugees who cannot have their own basic needs met and are not empowered to meet them themselves in their asylum country.

The rights that should be guaranteed to a refugee person become different when that person is seeking **Asylum (cf.)** and is living in the country that is processing his/her petition. Until the condition to become a refugee under the law's prescriptions is declared by the authorities of the asylum country, the rights and freedoms of that person are very limited. The rights of refugee claimants **(cf. Refugee Claimant)** are based on the state's obligation to preserve the dignity of the claimant while quickly and fairly processing their claim. Reducing the processing time of the claim is directly related to the ability to live a life with rights and freedom, since before refugee **Status (cf.)** is declared the person is in a state of suspended or limited freedom. They are physically living in the asylum country but they are substantially restricted in their personal activities: they cannot work, study, or satisfy their family's needs, including schooling for their children. They are living in **Limbo (cf.)**; their entity is pending.

National legislation should ensure that these rights can be exercised in the country of asylum, while the asylum state must develop policies and laws to guarantee the effective exercise of refugee rights. Further, they must protect refugees against racist and xenophobic acts **(cf. Racism)**, and condemn and effectively punish the perpetrators of such crimes openly. Such safeguarding requires that authorities make sure that all refugees are aware of their rights; that systems are put in place to look into refugees's issues; and that public campaigns creating awareness of refugee rights and promoting the values of human rights, respect, and protections, are clearly established as a cornerstone of the rule of law. At the same time, refugees have certain duties and must observe the laws and regulations of their asylum country.

il·le·gal
im·mi·grant

# Marianela Fuertes

A person who enters into and/or remains in a country without a valid visa or travel permit (with or without fraudulent documentation) is an illegal immigrant.

People who have been found not to qualify for **Asylum (cf.)** and therefore are not given refugee **Status (cf.)** have no right to remain within a signatory country under the terms of the **1951 Refugee Convention (cf.)**. Should they remain in the host country after this decision is passed, they become, by default, illegal immigrants.

# I

## Shiva Nourpanah

Integration may be thought of as a desirable outcome in the sense that successful immigration leads to refugees becoming fully integrated in their host society, but the term also refers to the process of integration. Integration may take place along economic, political, social, cultural, and/or psychological lines. Gaining **Citizenship (cf.)** or voting rights is generally seen as a sign of full political integration, while getting a job or buying property are examples of economic integration. It is possible to be, or feel "integrated" in some respects, yet not in others.

**Barriers (cf.)** to integration may include complex issues like racial discrimination **(cf. Racism)**, poverty, language barriers, and cuts to government funding that leave social services overstretched and unable to adequately address refugee needs. Integration is a dynamic, two-way process in which refugees and members of their host society learn from each other and show mutual respect and understanding. However, for any form of integration to take place, governments need to put in place strong supports **(cf. Settlement Services)**, recognizing the barriers and marginalization that refugees face as they settle into their new communities. The refugee process itself acts as a barrier to integration, keeping refugee claimants in **Limbo (cf.)**, unsure about their futures and in an extended state of anxiety and instability. Other policies, such as the lack of formal English-language classes for refugees in Nova Scotia, also exacerbate the situation.

# I

## Marianela Fuertes

Internally displaced individuals or groups of people are those who have been forced to escape or leave their home or territory of residence. Their leaving often occurs as they strive to avoid the effects of armed conflict, situations of widespread violence, or systemic human rights violations in their own country **(cf. Human & Refugee Rights)**. Though they are fleeing their homes, these displaced people have not left their country or crossed any international border; hence they are *internally* displaced.

In such cases the international human rights system considers the national authorities to have the primary duty and responsibility to provide assistance to displaced populations. The intervention of international organizations must be the result of a decision by the UN Secretary General, with the consent of the state where the assistance is needed.

Due to the rapid spread of armed conflict and the increase of authoritarian regimes, the number of internally displaced people has soared. The international human rights system has to recognize the problem and design a better and more efficient system to provide assistance to the internally displaced—not only for humanitarian reasons, but to prevent an increase in the already massive international migration of people in present day.

jour·ney

# Benjamin Amaya

The travel itineraries of refugees are typically much more complicated than a timely departure followed by a smooth arrival. Leaving the home country may be preceded, for many refugees, by years of **Internal Displacement (cf.)**, and travelling to Canada is often subsequent to prolonged temporary asylum in another country. Once in Canada, the start of a new life requires overcoming significant economic, social, and psychological obstacles, which may take years.

Since the beginning of Canada's refugee programs, examples of prolonged journeys abound. Among the most common ordeals refugees experience when embarking on their journeys are: living in environments of open warfare, forceful eviction from their homes, the loss of relatives and friends, witnessing and experiencing torture, the absence of basic government services such as health and education, family disintegration, and the loss of a sense of control and trust in people that results after trauma. The impact of these excruciating circumstances, while providing a strong motivation for **Resettlement (cf.)**, represents a significant burden that extends through the journey process and often for long periods afterwards.

# Julie Chamagne

It is always awe-inspiring to bear witness to the journeys that people have taken across the world and the different ways they have been able to get here. A journey to Canada might mean walking alongside your eight-year-old son, with your two-year-old daughter strapped to your back and a few earthly possessions in a bag, from Kosovo to Macedonia, in a group of hundreds, and then being airlifted out to a military base in Nova Scotia. It might be a solitary, terrifying container ship–ride across the Atlantic during which you are hiding out, praying that the crew doesn't find you and throw you overboard. It might involve many different modes of transportation and take you through dozens of countries. It might mean you use your life savings to buy a ticket and a passport, get on a plane in West Africa, transit through Europe, and land at the Halifax airport, where you approach the customs officers with trepidation and tell them your story. It might be a journey that starts as a trip overseas for your studies after high school; you say goodbye to your parents and set off for your new adult life, without knowing that in a few months war will break out and you will never return to your birthplace again.

When we think of refugees, we think of travel and migration, but the word "journey" can hold so many meanings.

Most people who do not experience an insider's view of the situation assume that the journey ends when a refugee reaches Canadian soil—but it is just the beginning of a different kind of journey. For **Refugee Claimants (cf.)**, the journey has just begun, and the next few years will likely be a journey to navigate complicated and oppressive systems and processes, which will culminate in a final decision on their **Status (cf.)**. There is the journey to **Permanent Residence (cf.)** and **Citizenship (cf.)** for people who are granted protection, and the journey of their family members to reunite with them here **(cf. Family Reunification)**, but there is also the heartbreaking and perilous journey back home, having being denied status **(cf. Repatriation)**.

# leg·is·la·tion

## Shiva Nourpanah

Most countries have put a range of laws, parliamentary acts, and regulations in place to manage refugee affairs in an orderly and lawful manner. These laws may change from time to time as governments with different ideologies and political leanings are elected and try to pass new legislation. Such changes may have ripple effects in the lives of refugees and service providers as they struggle to keep up with changing bureaucracies and procedures.

National legislation creates the legal infrastructure that determines how refugees are treated and what sorts of rights and protections they receive. It determines whether, and the extent to which, states implement the international instruments to which they are party. Canada has robust refugee legislation in place. It signed the **1951 Refugee Convention and the Protocol of 1967 (cf.)** in 1969, making the protection of refugees part of its international obligations.

The Immigration Act, the first piece of immigration legislation that recognized refugees, came into force in Canada in 1978. However, it is worth noting that refugee affairs are not legislated through immigration laws in all countries: many countries do not have a comparable immigration system to Canada, which has historically relied on immigration for economic development and "nation-building."

In 1981, the Private Sponsorship of Refugees Program was launched. In 1985, the Supreme Court of Canada recognized that **Refugee Claimants (cf.)** are entitled to fundamental justice under the Canadian Charter of Rights and Freedoms, and are entitled to the same basic **Human Rights (cf.)** as Canadian citizens. This paved the way for refugee reform and the establishing of the Immigration and Refugee Board of Canada (IRB), which began work in 1989. All quasi-judicial immigration matters in Canada are now handled by the IRB.

In 2002, the Immigration and Refugee Protection Act (IRPA) was passed. IRPA stated clearly that the refugee program is first and foremost about protection; that it reflects Canada's humanitarian traditions; that fairness and efficiency are important values to the nation; and that social and economic support of refugees and their families is vital to successful **Integration (cf.)** in their new communities. However, reflecting the post-9/11 concern with border security, front-end screening for refugee claimants intensified and tightened criminal inadmissibility. Appeal rights in cases of serious criminal exclusions were removed, and the process for obtaining national security certificates, already criticized for its lack of transparency by refugee advocates, was streamlined.[31]

In 2012, the controversial Bill C-31, also known as Protecting Canada's Immigration System Act, amended certain parts of

---

[31] Security certificates are issued by the federal government under IRPA in cases where a foreign national or permanent resident is deemed to be a threat to public safety and national security. It allows the Canadian Border Services Agency to remove that person from Canada. For further information, refer to https://www.publicsafety.gc.ca/cnt/ntnl-scrt/cntr-trrrsm/scrt-crtfcts-en.aspx.

IRPA. These changes implemented hasty timelines, denying refugees a fair chance to prove their claims, fewer rights for claimants coming from "designated countries of origin," mandatory detention for certain categories of claimants, and in general, fewer rights in the refugee determination system. Parts of the Interim Federal Healthcare Plan (IFHP) for refugees were removed, causing great outcry. Strong refugee activism and solidarity **(cf. Activism & Advocacy)** from other health-care sectors eventually led to the restoration of the IFHP, though not before great harm was done to the health and well-being of many claimants **(cf. Health & Health Care)**.

Refugee legislation, in Canada and elsewhere, often becomes a political football, reflective of opportunistic and short-term goals rather than a genuine and sustained humanitarian commitment to the cause of refugees. Activists and civil society always need to be vigilant and responsive to changes in refugee-related legislation, as these rights can be easily lost in turbulent social and political times.

# L

## Shiva Nourpanah

Waiting has become an inherent yet often overlooked part of the reality of the refugee experience. As one of the most vulnerable and powerless groups in society, refugees are easily ignored, and their affairs shunted to the bottom of the pile in an era of competing demands. Lacking the voice and power of "regular" citizens, with the threat of **Deportation (cf.)** always hanging over them, refugees experience long waiting times in a variety of harsh conditions.

Refugees speak passionately about the waiting they endure in their countries of refuge. The condition of limbo—of not knowing whether you can live as a regular citizen, with all the associated rights and responsibilities, of knowing that you may be deported and returned to the place you fled—is a stressor not often mentioned in policies. It has long-term impacts on future settlement prospects, and affects refugee children as well as adults. It may lead to or exacerbate mental health issues, complicating the development of a healthy sense of belonging and stability and hindering the ability to move past and heal from the experiences leading to their flight.

In Canada, wait times currently hover around two years, from the moment a claim is made to the final decision. Refugees with more complicated cases may expect wait times of five years or more. Cruelly, there are instances where an interview is scheduled only to be cancelled at short notice—even the day before. The surge of emotions can be hard to manage.

Long periods of waiting may be also embedded in the **Journey (cf.)** itself: there are numerous testimonies of long wait times in strange cities, in uncertain and often impoverished circumstances, as refugees wait for the arrangements of their onward travel to be finalized. They remain hidden and discreet, in small motels at the edge of urban life, waiting to be collected by the smugglers to whom they have entrusted their life and family savings **(cf. Smuggling)**. At these moments, they are particularly vulnerable to arrest, fraud, and other forms of abuse.

Finally, for some refugees born in camps or as urban refugees, waiting is all they have ever known. Iran, Pakistan, and Kenya are some of the countries that have refugee populations who settled in "temporary" camps that have persisted for over thirty years. Births, weddings, and deaths take place in these mini-towns, some with their own markets and money systems in place, and complicated arrangements with "locals." They have slipped from the media spotlight. Their younger generations grow up never having known their home country, and carry on the waiting and hoping for the stability and secure lives that have eluded their parents.

# Evangelia Tastsoglou

Migration has historically always been part of the human experience. It refers to the movement and settlement of people from one location to another within a state, between states, or across states. This movement can be voluntary or forced, permanent or temporary, cyclical or transnational. Thus, a migrant is a person who: moves from their country of origin or residence to another country to permanently settle (immigrant); moves and settles from their country of origin or residence to another country temporarily for work or study purposes (temporary migrant or international student); moves and settles from their country of origin or residence to seek protection that they could not access in their state of citizenship or residence (refugee, person in need of protection, or refugee claimant); moves back and forth between two states for work or other purposes (cyclical migrant); moves across several states for work, study, protection, or other purposes or, though moved and settled in a different state from the country of origin or former residence, is in ongoing contact, via travel and electronic communication, with their former country of origin or residence (transnational migrant). The category of **Forced Migrant (cf.)** includes refugees and others needing protection, refugee claimants, and asylum seekers.

# non-re·foule·ment

## Marianela Fuertes

The principle of non-refoulement is the cornerstone of refugee protection, enshrined in the basic articles of the Geneva Convention, which states: "No contracting State shall expel or return (*"refouler"*) a refugee in any manner whatsoever to the frontiers of territories where their life or freedom would be threatened on account of race, religion, nationality, membership of a particular social group or political opinion."

In the **1951 Refugee Convention (cf.)**, Article 33(1), non-refoulement is defined as an essential principle of international law in relation to refugees and asylum seekers that protects against their return to a country where the person has reason to fear persecution.[32]

The asylum country is not able to restrict this prohibition of non-refoulement through its own legislation or regulations. The only exceptions to this prohibition permitted in Canada are:

---

[32] UN General Assembly, *Convention Relating to the Status of Refugees*.

2  *(a) [W]ho is inadmissible on grounds of serious criminality and who constitutes, in the opinion of the Minister, a danger to the public in Canada; or*

3  *(b) [W]ho is inadmissible on grounds of security, violating human or international rights or organized criminality if, in the opinion of the Minister, the person should not be allowed to remain in Canada on the basis of the nature and severity of acts committed or of danger to the security of Canada.[33]*

[33] National Legislative Bodies / National Authorities. *Canada: Immigration and Refugee Protection Act (IRPA)*, (2001), https://www.refworld.org/docid/4f0dc8f12.html.

# per·ma·nent res·i·dence

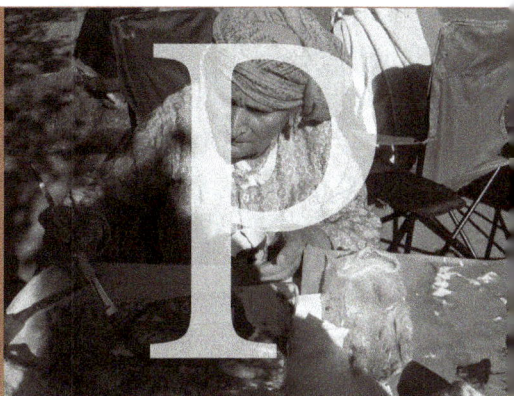

## Shiva Nourpanah

Permanent residence applies to a **Status (cf.)** of immigrants and refugees who are allowed to live legally and securely in a country, but who do not have the full rights and responsibilities of **Citizenship (cf.)**. For example, permanent residents in Canada are not allowed to vote in elections, run for political office, or obtain Canadian passports. With the permanent resident card in hand, they can leave Canada and re-enter legally. Those who have entered and lived in Canada on a temporary status, such as international students, **Refugee Claimants (cf.)**, and those who are seeking to stay in Canada on humanitarian and compassionate grounds, will also need to apply and be granted permanent residence if they intend to continue living in Canada permanently. If and when the claim of a refugee is recognized by the Immigration and Refugee Board of Canada (IRB) they will need to apply and obtain permanent residence as the next step on the path to citizenship. Applications are costly, and the high fees, which can quickly climb to thousands of dollars per family, are often a major deterrent.

The term "permanent" is deceptive. In Canada, permanent residencies have to be renewed every five years. One of the conditions of renewing permanent residence is that the applicant must have resided in Canada for a total of two years of the preceding five years. Permanent residents, under certain circumstances, may be deported from Canada. However, applying for permanent residency renewal is generally much easier and less costly than applying for citizenship, and so it may happen that people remain permanent residents for years, without taking the daunting step of becoming a citizen. In normal circumstances, permanent residents may feel this might not make such a huge difference in their lives, especially if they already hold the citizenship of a country which they feel can offer them reliable protection, should they require it. For refugees who have lost the protection of their country of origin, remaining on permanent residence without obtaining citizenship may prove to have serious consequences should circumstances go awry.

A notorious case that attracted the attention of refugee activists is that of Abdoul Abdi, who arrived in Nova Scotia as a child refugee from Somalia. He grew up as a permanent resident in the Nova Scotia childcare system, which failed to obtain his citizenship at a time when he would have become eligible. As a young adult, Abdi committed crimes which, lacking the protection of citizenship, would have resulted in his deportation back to Somalia—a country he had fled in childhood. However the 2018 public outcry and activism at this clear miscarriage of justice resulted in a pause of the **Deportation (cf.)** proceedings. Abdi remains in Canada, subject to criminal justice proceedings here, rather than being punished twice.

# per·se·cu·tion

P

## Katie Tinker

Persecution is at the heart of our understanding of what makes someone a **Refugee (cf.)**. Our national and international laws and conventions tell us that it is because of persecution that refugees must flee their homes, and because of the risk of persecution that they are offered protection in other countries. Yet, interestingly, the word "persecution" is never actually defined in the **1951 Refugee Convention (cf.)**, and it remains undefined in Canada's own Immigration and Refugee Protection Act (IRPA).

According to the Immigration and Refugee Board (IRB) of Canada's own guideline paper, the legal understanding of persecution has evolved over time, as various cases have gone before the courts. Gradually, we have identified some key elements which are deemed necessary in order to conclude that someone's experience amounts to persecution. For example, the harm they experienced, or that they fear experiencing, must amount to more than discrimination or harassment. It must deny the victim his or her basic dignity and **Human Rights (cf.)**. It must be linked to one of the 1951 Refugee Convention grounds. And the experience will in many instances be systematic and repetitive (e.g. a woman who suffers repeated incidents of domestic violence at the hands of her partner). These parameters are not absolute. For example, some isolated experiences have been recognized to be so terrible that they do not need to be repeated more than once to be considered persecutory (e.g. a person whose family member was killed in order to punish them, or someone who was arrested a single time and severely tortured). Some persecutory acts—notably female genital mutilation—are systematic in that they are carried out repeatedly against a particular group within society, and their consequences are experienced repeatedly over time, even if the individual will only experience the act itself once **(cf. Gender)**.

Sadly, it is likely precisely because there are so many different ways in which people persecute one another that the term has proved challenging to define. And as history marches on, we will no doubt witness new and unimagined forms of oppression and trauma, and our definition of persecution will be forced to expand even more to accommodate them.

# rac·ism

# Sylvia Calatayud, Huwaida Medani, & Shiva Nourpanah

Racism is discrimination against people of colour. It ensures that one racial group has and maintains power and privilege over all others, in all aspects of life, at the expense of other racial groups. It is measured by economic, cultural, sociological, and political outcomes rather than its intentions, and may occur in three different forms.

*Institutional racism* is created and maintained by economic, political, and social institutions, as well as cultural relations.

*Interpersonal racism* refers to the behaviour and actions among individuals or groups that reinforce the views of the dominant economic, cultural, sociological, and/or political paradigm, regardless of the individual's good intentions. An individual may act in a racist manner unintentionally but still impact the racialized group.

Ways of thinking and behaving on the part of racialized people that contribute to their own oppression by reinforcing a dominant economic, cultural, sociological, and/or political paradigm is sometimes called *internalized racism*.[34]

It is worth noting that many people believe that racialized people cannot be racist because their racialization will take away all racial benefits. When racialized people make harsh or prejudiced statements against white people or engage in prejudiced actions, this reflects hostile attitudes toward white people, but such attitudes must be distinguished from systemic control over the lives/lifestyles of white people. Although bias and prejudice within racialized groups clearly exist, the ultimate outcome is to prop up racist/oppressive systems of control.

Refugees who come from racialized backgrounds often experience all these forms of discrimination and aggression. Indeed racial discrimination, sometimes overtly expressed as racial hatred, and sometimes as simple ignorance, is one of the **Barriers (cf.)** to successful **Integration (cf.)**.

Scholars have argued that racial discrimination is systematically embedded in the whole immigration and refugee system, both internationally and nationally within Canada. This could be deemed an understatement, since Canada's immigration policy specifically excluded non-whites, and was designed to attract only Europeans, from the early twentieth century up to 1976. With the passing of the Canadian Multiculturalism Act under Pierre Trudeau's government in 1988, explicit racial bias was removed

---

[34]These definitions are adapted from the work of Louise Derman-Sparks and Carol Brunson Phillips, published in *Teaching/Learning Anti-Racism: A Developmental Approach* (New York: Teachers College Press, 1997).

from Canadian immigration policy. Nevertheless, legislation such as Protecting Canada's Immigration System Act or Bill C-31 (2012), which introduced stricter measures around refugee **Detention (cf.)** and **Deportation (cf.)**, provoked criticism from organizations such as Human Rights Watch and Amnesty International. The Canadian government was accused of subjecting refugees, often from developing or underdeveloped countries, who were ethnic minorities in Canada, to treatment that would be wholly unacceptable to its own citizenry.

# R

ref·u·gee

## Marianela Fuertes

The response to the persecution of certain groups and the decision to consider them refugees happens through an ethical and political judgment highly intertwined with the historical context and present government power of a nation. The origin of the "classic refugee" arose from the religious persecution inherent in the process of consolidation of the European monarchies. The conflict between Catholics and Protestants, for example, produced massive persecutions. In the context of absolutism, religious persecution was one of the principal elements used to define and consolidate governmental power.

The refugee process requires a government or authority on the other side that grants refugees asylum and protection. To generate the refugee **Status (cf.)**, some conditions have to be present in the **Country of Origin (cf.)** from which they flee, and recognition of need has to occur in the country of destination. This dual dynamic is fundamental to the evolution of the meaning of the term "refugee." While the definition has changed over time, a consensus was established in the **1951 Refugee Convention (cf.)**, identifying a person who is under well-founded fear of being persecuted for one or more of the five grounds listed in Article 1 A(2) ( race, religion, nationality, membership of a particular social group, or political opinion), and so is forced to look for protection outside his/her country. In addition to these five grounds, other consistent reasons to seek asylum include all fears of being subject to cruel or degrading treatment that constitute torture or human rights violations according with the UN Convention against Torture (UNCAT).

The definition of "refugee" has been developed under some dichotomous tensions that have defined the main characteristics of the concepts that international law applies today. It is useful to mention these tensions because they are a fundamental part of the methodology, as well the dynamic, by which the answer to the question "Who is a refugee?" is created.

## Dichotomy 1: Between core universal humanitarian values and strategic national decisions.

Presently, the international system to assist refugees is based on the universal principle of human rights that everybody deserves protection. At the same time, the states that are part of the international system continue to exercise important discretion in implementing the definition and interpreting their obligations to define their internal policies for refugees.

## Dichotomy 2: Between economic and political displacement.

There are many historical examples of economics and politics intertwining to produce bloody confrontations, deep fractures, and cruel persecutions. In bad times the only alternative to starvation was emigration. In the present, the large displacement crisis suggests that the individual, involuntary political emergency approach to providing protection is insufficient to providing effective humanitarian aid.

Humanitarian programs have been developed out of the need to address major international crises and so the international system intervenes in matters of natural disasters, economic crises, and political persecution in line with the universal principle of human rights protection. But refugee crises are distinguished from other kinds of catastrophic humanitarian crises, and so international organizations have to count on those countries who have the power to exercise their own sovereignty and design their own immigration policies in a particular international context.

These are just some of the tensions that frame the humanitarian response to providing aid to hundreds of people who suffer inhumane conditions in a world organized through sovereign states. Now, in the twenty-first century, the situation is more complex than ever. The increasing number of internal armed conflicts, natural disasters, pandemics, and an integrated economy that speeds up the consequences of any crisis, leaving hundreds without jobs or basic income, are just a few of the contemporary situations that complicate and threaten to expand the definition of a refugee.

Reactions to the refugee crisis have created nationalistic movements and strained political systems, such as the European Union dealing with Brexit and a popular perception of the crisis as an invasion by potential terrorists. This particular movement shows how instead of a humanitarian response to the refugee crisis, the public reaction has been to turn away from globalism in favour of asserting the integrity of the nation state.

## Dichotomy 3: Between universal protection of human rights and national identity.

Sovereignty has been built as an expression of autonomous governance in the current world formed by states that have an important function to protect and promote the common good of their citizens, and in that sense the state has a legitimate authority to restrict the freedom of the non-citizens to enter the country. Reasons like crime prevention, epidemics, national security, economic stability, and maintaining peace are some of the motivations that inspire immigration restrictions.

The main issues around immigration have to do with the number of people allowed entry to affluent countries. "What is too much immigration?" seems to be the point of tension in all discussions that at the same time have a variety of motivations and fears. The immigration policies that get more favourable opinion are those that impose fewer demands on the taxpayers. The local citizenry may be willing to support the immigration of people who will be productive members of the community and contribute more in the way of taxes than the cost they impose on the community in terms of education, health care, unemployment, public housing, law enforcement, and social-welfare expenditures. Thus, professionals are preferred over anyone who will need social investment, such as youth, seniors, and refugees.

The refugee crisis specifically has inspired nationalistic movements and strained political systems in response, such as the European Union's dealing with Brexit and Trump's anti-immigration campaigns. The extreme portrayal of immigrants and refugees as potential terrorists is just one of the ways in which the public reaction has been to turn away from globalism and humanitarianism and return to asserting the integrity of the nation state. The question is, when does the international community have the duty to provide asylum?

## The Convention definition and the refugee crisis in the twenty-first century.

The Convention definition of refugee has made less sense as the nature of the issue has changed and the numbers have risen. Since 1980, refugee movements have been more likely to be the result of civil wars, ethnic and communal conflicts, generalized violence, natural disasters, and famine—usually in combination—than of individually targeted persecution by an oppressive regime.[35]

A renewed focus on human rights is part of the interpretation movement that has afforded protection to people in situations that did not fit into the five entry points of the 1951 Convention definition of refugee. The Organization of African Unity (OAU) Refugee Convention, adopted in 1969, added the following to the original definition: "Any person compelled to leave his/ her country owing to external aggression, occupation, foreign domination or even serious disturbing public order in either part or the whole of his country of origin or nationality." In 1984 the Latin American countries added more objective considerations to the definition: "Any person who flees their country because life, safety or freedom have been threatened by generalized violence, foreign aggression, internal conflict, massive violation

---

[35] UNHCR has acknowledged the need for restrictive measures and sped up determination processes, while simultaneously criticizing governments for blocking access to possibly genuine refugees.

of human rights or other circumstances which have seriously disturbed public order."[36]

On the other hand, the non-refoulement prohibition of the 1951 Convention and the Convention against Torture (UNCAT) have been created as the basis to acknowledge a different spectrum of circumstances that compel people to seek asylum beyond the five entry grounds. Thus, people seeking asylum due to persecution for their gender, for example, have gotten protection even though they are not recognized as a refugee according with the 1951 Convention when returning them to their own country would put their life, safety, or freedom in serious danger. Thus returning asylum seekers to their country of origin would go against the *Universal Declaration of Human Rights* and the non-refoulement prohibition.

These are just some of the new elements that affect the definition of the term "refugee" and the decision to grant asylum. There are many who call for a new definition of refugee and changes to the 1951 Convention, however until that complex process sees light, the priority of human rights and protection against inhumane and degrading treatment give important opportunities for safety to those suffering persecution outside of the original five entry points that do not address the complexities of our twenty-first-century reality.

---

[36]UNHCR, *Handbook and Guidelines on Procedures and Criteria for Determining Refugee Status under the 1951 Convention and the 1967 Protocol Relating to the Status of Refugees*, December 2011, https://www.refworld.org/docid/4f33c8d92.html.

# R

ref·u·gee
claim·ant

## Marianela Fuertes

"Refugee claimant" is the term used in Canadian law to identify the person who is seeking **Asylum (cf.)**. The concept of a refugee claimant is defined by the terms of the **1951 Refugee Convention (cf.)** as someone who is seeking protection from persecution for one of the five grounds listed in Article 1A(2): the person is forced to flee his/her home due to persecution for reasons of race, religion, nationality, membership of particular social group, or political opinions. Also due to risk to their life, risk of cruel, inhuman or degrading treatment, or danger of torture where the person is unavailable to avail himself of the protection of that country.

The terms "refugee claimant" and "asylum seeker" are often misunderstood and used incorrectly to refer to people who have migrated for economic reasons **(cf. Economic Migrant)**, those who have had to leave their home but do not leave the country **(cf. Internal Displacement)**, or victims of a massive natural disaster.

# ref·u·gee
## sur place

# R

# Shiva Nourpanah

Sometimes upheavals and reversals can happen so suddenly that people are caught unawares. Countries that had been peaceful may become conflict zones almost overnight, or a change in the political regime may result in persecution and danger for families who had been living in relative security. In such circumstances, family members who have been travelling abroad—perhaps on business, or to study—may find themselves unable to return to their home country. Those who find themselves in such unfortunate situations are termed "refugees sur place."

Although the international community recognizes that these situations exist, and that the people caught in them require protection just as much as those who have fled from their countries in fear of persecution, refugees sur place may face different kinds of challenges. Generally, they do not look like "typical" refugees and victims of war and persecution. For example, they may be financially comfortable, having originally travelled in conditions of relative ease and security. They may not bear obvious marks of trauma and suffering. They will most likely be carrying the official passport issued by their home government, with the implication that they should be protected by that government when they are overseas. The only evidence of persecution may come second-hand, through warnings by friends and families, therefore lacking the weight of direct documentation.

Nevertheless, the experience of suddenly realizing that the place you call home has become dangerous, that you can no longer return as you were planning to when your visit draws to an end, and that you need to plan for your temporary stay to become longer and even permanent, has its own challenges. Mentally, emotionally, financially, and legally, refugees sur place undergo a unique and specific experience of the hardships of refuge.

Over the years, Atlantic Canada has witnessed a growing number of such refugees, namely international students from countries in the Middle East or Africa who have found themselves unable to return to their home countries due to sudden and unforeseen political changes. These students have good prospects for **Integration (cf.)**, since they are not facing the **Barriers (cf.)** that "typical" refugee claimants have. They will most likely have strong language skills, higher education, good employment prospects, and a network of connections established through their university studies. Nevertheless, this is no guarantee that they will be able to make a successful refugee claim.

# re·pa·tri·a·tion

# R

# Shiva Nourpanah

It may happen that the conditions that created a refugee flow changes for the better. Wars end, peace flourishes, and the people who once had to flee their homes and villages may wish to return and rebuild their lives. In such circumstances, repatriation, literally meaning "return to the homeland," offers a desirable and durable solution for refugees.

Repatriation can take place spontaneously and informally. However, in some circumstances, international agencies set up formal, planned repatriation operations. These operations ensure that repatriation takes place with security and dignity, and that refugees are not forced to return to places that may still be dangerous to them. Repatriation must be undertaken voluntarily by refugees, since returning people against their wish to places where they may be subject to danger is a violation of their **Human Rights (cf.)**. Thus, it is important to distinguish voluntary repatriation from the arbitrary arrests, forced deportations, and refoulements to which governments have sometimes subjected the refugee populations in their territory. In formal voluntary repatriation operations, representatives of **UNHCR (cf.)** work with the governments of the sending and receiving countries, as well as the refugees who have chosen to return, to ensure that repatriation is conducted in safe, dignified, and voluntary circumstances. Aid packages may be handed to returning refugees to provide a little help on their journey home and toward their efforts to rebuild their lives.

One of the largest formal voluntary repatriation operations spearheaded by UNHCR took place from Iran and Pakistan to Afghanistan from 2000 onwards. This was a widely-publicized attempt to find a solution to the plight of over 1 million Afghan refugees who had been stranded in those countries since the 1970s. These refugees had no hope of ever being formally accepted and **Integrated (cf.)** into their countries of refuge, and the vast majority of them had no chance of moving on and establishing themselves elsewhere. Even though the situation in Afghanistan remained volatile, it was thought calm enough to allow for repatriation to certain areas, though most of the southern provinces remained out of bounds. Twenty years on, voluntary repatriation to a country that remains one of the most prolific refugee-producing regions in the world remains controversial and problematic.

# re·set·tle·ment

R

## Shiva Nourpanah

When refugees have no foreseeable hope of returning to their home country, and local integration into their current country of refuge is not considered a viable solution, resettlement may be considered. Resettlement is a delicate operation through which certain selected refugees are given the option to move to a **Safe Third Country (cf.)**, the "resettlement country," in a legal, secure manner, with the expectation of gaining permanent residence and citizenship in the reasonable future. Resettlement usually takes place from a country of **Asylum (cf.)** rather than the refugee's home country, though under certain exceptional circumstances, refugees have been directly resettled from their home country.

Annually, several hundred refugees may be resettled to various countries whose governments have committed to accepting them. The main resettlement countries are the USA, Canada, Australia, and Sweden. The governments of these countries send officers from their relevant agency to countries of asylum, often through liaison with **UNHCR (cf.)** and/or other agencies such as the International Organization for Migration (IOM). They interview refugees who have already been pre-screened and assessed as meeting the **1951 Refugee Convention (cf.)** definition of a **Refugee (cf.)**, and further deemed to meet certain resettlement categories, rendering them eligible for resettlement. Commonly used resettlement categories include "Women at Risk" and "Legal and Physical Protection Needs." Countries have different sets of conditions for accepting refugees for resettlement, and the bureaucracy for gaining final admission can be very lengthy—up to several years in more complex cases. Once refugees are accepted for resettlement, they may face further bureaucratic hurdles when they try to exit their country of asylum and/or enter their safe third country. Upon arrival, they are met by service provision agencies that assist them with settlement and integration in the new community **(cf. Settlement Services)**.

Given that UNHCR's latest figures report a staggering total of 68.5 million forcibly displaced people **(cf. Forced Migration)**, it is understandable why resettlement may be dismissed as a mere token gesture of good will by wealthy countries towards vulnerable refugee populations. Nevertheless, it is an important tool that addresses the needs of some of the most vulnerable sections of refugee populations, and makes real change to their situation, while bringing visibility to their cause. It should be criticized for not doing enough, but it should not be discarded as useless.

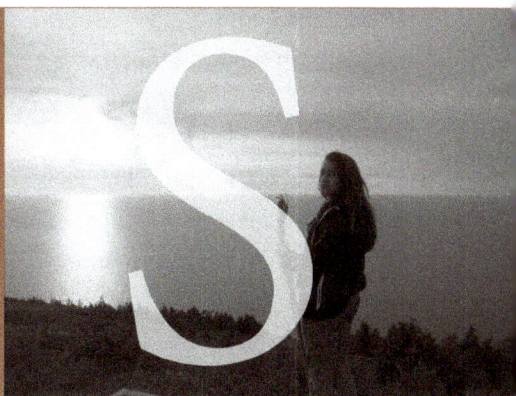

## safe third coun·try

# Katie Tinker

The Canada–United States Safe Third Country Agreement (STCA) is a formal agreement between the two nations which states that citizens of other countries who wish to request **Asylum (cf.)** in Canada or the US must do so in the first place that they arrive. The agreement, which came into force in December 2004, is based on an official understanding that both countries offer refugees similar and adequate protection and a fair process for those fleeing **Persecution (cf.)** to request such protection. Its stated aim is to give both governments a greater ability to regulate and control movements of refugee populations within North America.

The agreement is in force at all official land border crossings between Canada and the US, as well as at international airports. Only those who meet the requirements for certain exceptions to the agreement, including **Unaccompanied Minors (cf.)**, and those who entered one country but have a relative in the other, are allowed to enter from the US into Canada, or vice versa, for the purpose of asking for protection.

Many Canadians have criticized the agreement since its inception, primarily on the basis that the assumption of fair protection for refugees in the US is problematic. A legal challenge against the agreement was launched in 2005 by several parties, including the Canadian Council for Refugees and Amnesty International; the challenge was initially upheld, but later overturned by the Canadian Federal Court of Appeal.

In recent years, several anti-immigration policies enacted by the administration of US president Donald Trump have led to renewed and urgent calls by refugee advocates to suspend or discontinue the STCA. Trump's most controversial measures have included: a blanket ban on entry into the US by citizens of several Muslim-majority countries; a significant clawing back of the US's refugee resettlement program; an announcement in June 2018 that refugees fleeing domestic violence and gang violence would no longer be eligible for protection in the US; the automatic detention of adult asylum seekers entering the US; and the deeply troubling practice of forcibly separating parents and children who have crossed the US's southern border in search of safety. These events have led many to argue that the US is no longer meeting its obligations under several international agreements pertaining to refugees, children, and human rights, and that it can no longer be considered a safe country by the Canadian government. Some feel it is only a matter of time before the agreement is struck down by the courts for being unconstitutional under the Canadian Charter of Rights and Freedoms.

In practice, the existence of the STCA in the context of an anti-immigration administration in the US presents another legal and ethical dilemma for Canada. Knowing or perceiving that they are unlikely to be allowed to remain in the US, but aware that they will not be allowed to enter Canada at an official border, many asylum seekers are choosing to take the risky step of crossing the border into Canada outside its official entry points. While Canada may have the jurisdiction to refuse these individuals entry at the border, once they are inside Canada, the STCA effectively no longer applies to them. They cannot be sent back across the border to the US without the US agreeing to take them back, nor can they be returned to their home country without first being granted a chance to ask for protection in Canada. Since the election of Donald Trump, the number of people crossing into Canada from the US without permission has increased so sharply that it has led to a significant backlog in cases waiting to be heard by the Immigration and Refugee Board of Canada (IRB). These delays are a source of great stress to those waiting for their cases to be decided—particularly those who cannot apply to bring family members to join them until they know whether their claims will be accepted.

Stephen, who has asked that his last name not be used for privacy reasons, is a **Refugee Claimant (cf.)** in Canada who crossed the border from the US in the spring of 2018 with his wife and three daughters. He agreed to speak about his experience for this publication. Stephen and his family left Nigeria and came to the US as visitors because they feared for the safety of the girls. "We knew even before we arrived what Trump was saying," he said. "But for us it was still better than Nigeria."

However, soon after the family arrived, Stephen's sister-in-law, who was living in the US, told them it was worse than they expected, and that they should think about going to Canada in order to avoid being deported from the US. "We went online that same night, the night we arrived, and found videos and advice on going to Canada," Stephen said. "We didn't sleep that night, thinking about it. We felt that there was an urgency because of so many people crossing. We worried that soon they might close the border."

Stephen and his family travelled just days later. He recalls that going across the border was stressful, but adds that he felt that it would be okay for them in the end because there were many people besides them crossing over at the same time, and because he knew Canada was a good country that treated immigrants well. Stephen and his family were unaware of the STCA when they arrived here, and in fact did not even realize it would have been possible to claim asylum in the US. They were simply acting according to the information they were able to glean from others in their position.

"If you have an issue, and there was a way to stay in America, it would be good," he says. "But when you hear Trump saying he doesn't want this group, that group—people start running."

# set·tle·ment serv·ices

# San Patten

The term "settlement services" refers to the full range of supports provided to newcomers by governments and non-governmental organizations to help them establish a new life in their place of settlement. Ideally, these supports help newcomers gain equal access to opportunities and resources available to all citizens, participate meaningfully in society's economic, social, and political life, and generally help build and encourage feelings of belonging. Settlement services give newcomers access to both material and interpersonal determinants of health (both physical health and mental health). The material social determinants of health **(cf. Health & Health Care)** include safe living environments, adequate food and housing, high-quality health care, and appropriate employment. The interpersonal social determinants of health include experiences of social inclusion, protection against discrimination, cultural integration, and equal social status.

On a day-to-day basis, settlement-service providers help newcomers through a wide variety of supports, including (but not limited to):

- *Interpretation and translation of documents*
- *Filling out forms and applications (e.g., for income assistance)*
- *Language classes*
- *Employment assistance such as resumé writing, job hunting, job interview preparation, and pre-job training*
- *Referrals and information about other community services, schools, and health care*
- *Obtaining work and study permits*
- *Housing support for immediate, temporary, and long-term housing*
- *Accessing legal aid counsel for non-refugee legal matters*
- *Accessing mental health services and psychological counselling*
- *Accessing food banks, clothing, furniture, and other household basics*
- *Setting up bank accounts and utilities*
- *Providing or promoting free or low-cost educational opportunities related to life in Canada [37]*
- *Organizing social/recreational activities within the community*

Settlement services are usually provided by community organizations and non-governmental organizations (NGOs), such as the Halifax Refugee Clinic. NGOs are non-profit organizations,

---

[37] E.g., lectures and courses on subjects like tenant rights and responsibilities, government programs, community resources, the education system, computer literacy, and more.

institutionally separate from governments, governed by volunteer boards of directors. They are mission and values driven, and guided by strategic goals that contribute to quality of life in our communities. In the immigration- and refugee-serving sector, NGOs can act at local, provincial, regional, national, or international levels to provide assistance to **Migrants (cf.)** and newcomers, and to help protect their rights. These NGOs may provide assistance during the migration process, as well as after landing in destination countries, to help with the settlement process. Immigrant-serving agencies, multicultural and ethno-cultural groups, refugee legal clinics, immigrant or refugee health clinics, and advocacy organizations focused on public awareness and policy are all examples of NGOs engaged in the timely and equitable integration of newcomers.

Refugee claimants and asylum seekers are particularly reliant on NGOs for settlement assistance, as many are not eligible for other government-funded supports that are made available for language learning, housing, education, and health care, to immigrants and government-assisted refugees.

# Julie Chamagne

The staff at the Halifax Refugee Clinic have created a place of sanctuary and welcome for people who are fearing **Persecution (cf.)**. Leading through an intersectionally feminist, non-hierarchical structure is of paramount importance to create an environment where equity is the central priority. Like most core staff members in a small NGO, the key staff there fill many roles, and in the course of a day may give a media interview, meet a client for legal and settlement advice, and find emergency housing or make a cup of tea for newly-arrived clients.

# S

**smugg·ling**

## Shiva Nourpanah

Smuggling and **Trafficking (cf.)** are often conflated, and indeed the line between them may become quite blurred in real-life situations. International law, however, sets out the distinction quite clearly. In human smuggling, people consent to their movement and willingly pay their smugglers "market" rates to travel to safety and security. Traffickers, on the other hand, forcibly move people to places against their will, where they may be exploited for purposes such as working under illegal and/or dangerous conditions.

Many refugees describe using the services of professional human smugglers to arrange for their exit out of their country of origin and entrance into a safe country. They turn over substantial sums of money—often their life savings and family property—as payment, with no guarantees that they will successfully reach their destination **(cf. Journey)**. They endure long periods of waiting while their smugglers arrange their trips **(cf. Limbo)**. Many smugglers are unscrupulous criminals who have no hesitation in dumping refugees, or conning them out of their money, if the circumstances warrant it. Smuggling is a criminalized activity, carrying with it harsh penalties and sanctions.

It is also a flourishing business. Refugees describe smugglers selling voyages to every popular refugee destination in the streets of cities in Afghanistan and other refugee-producing countries. Though they are aware of the dangers and risks involved, refugees turn to smugglers due to their lack of legal options to leave dangerous conditions in safety and security. It is true that smugglers can be predatory and criminal, but they are offering much needed services. It is in their interest to ensure that their clients arrive safely and in one piece to their destination, and thus they attempt to arrange their trips efficiently, drawing as little attention as possible to themselves and their clients.

Smuggling occurs alongside the deep involvement of officialdom and government agents across the globe. Refugees describe being whisked through airports, passed through road checks and border points, and placed on boats, buses, and trucks with the brisk efficiency of experienced tour guides.

Government rhetoric criminalizing smugglers and blaming refugees for using them is hypocritical and disingenuous. A genuine desire to reduce the criminality associated with smuggling would involve developing better and safer legal options for refugees to leave dangerous and insecure conditions. Providing safe, transparent, and legal routes for refugees to seek asylum would effectively cut off the supply of clients to smugglers. On the other hand, continuing to criminalize smuggling merely exacerbates the dangers that refugees face, increases their vulnerability **(cf. Vulnerability & Resiliency)**, and worsens global corruption and organized crime.

# S  spon·sor·ship

## Wenche Gausdal

Nova Scotian communities have a long history of coming together to sponsor refugees, reunite families, and consciously build more welcoming and diverse communities. In 2015, with the support of the Canadian Refugee Sponsorship Agreement Holders Association (SAH), the settlement sector, and community resources, thousands of volunteers sponsored and settled Syrian families, enabling them to leave unsafe and difficult situations for a new life in Canada. In the process, those who sponsor gain a deep understanding of refugee family needs, the importance of building welcoming communities to foster a sense of belonging, and accessible language, settlement, employment, and health services.

Sponsors are important voices on refugee and immigration policies and on **Barriers (cf.)** to successful refugee resettlement. To keep this volunteer community active, more opportunities and resources to sponsor refugees are needed. Sponsorship Agreement Holders (SAH's), the settlement sector, and other organizations in host communities need resources to support them through the fundraising, sponsorship application, resettlement, and integration processes. Comprehensive support for these extraordinary volunteers is essential.

# state·less·ness & state pro·tec·tion

## Julie Chamagne

A fundamental notion in refugee law is that of state protection, or lack thereof. This means if a person fears **Persecution (cf.)**, they need to show that their state cannot protect them against that persecution. But what if that person does not even have a state? People who are stateless are in a unique position, in that they do not always fall under the definition of **Refugee (cf.)**.

The most prominent group of stateless people are the Palestinians: those who were forcibly removed from their land from 1948 onwards and became refugees around the world as well as those who continue to live in the occupied territories today with no right to **Citizenship (cf.)**. Stateless Palestinians make up more than half of the estimated 10 million stateless people around the world.

A person may be born stateless or become stateless. Issues between the conferral of nationality through the right of birth (*jus sanguinis*) or the right of soil (*jus soli*) is a cause of statelessness. Administrative and procedural **Barriers (cf.)** can contribute to statelessness, and sometimes different ethnic groups in countries are systematically excluded from nationality. People can also be rendered stateless when a jurisdiction ceases to exist. There is also a gendered aspect to statelessness, in that in many countries, nationality cannot be transmitted through the mother **(cf. Gender)**.

Stateless people are uniquely vulnerable and oppressed around the world for many reasons. They are often marginalized and lack basic rights in their country of residence. Their lack of ID and travel documents limits movement. They are vulnerable in Canada as well, as statelessness is not grounds for refugee protection and there is no specific determination procedure or legal framework for regularizing stateless people. Canada is not a signatory to the 1954 *Convention Relating to the Status of Stateless Persons*. This international **Human Rights (cf.)** instrument was designed to protect and improve the basic human rights and **Status (cf.)** of stateless people and deals with their access to education, employment, housing, and identity and travel documents.

# sta·tus

## Shiva Nourpanah

Like air, good health, and decent schools and roads, status in the context of immigration and citizenship is something we barely notice unless we have the misfortune of losing it. Status refers to the relationship of an individual and the state. The various civic, political, social, and economic rights that individuals may be granted in a particular territory depend on the degree to which the state governing that territory recognizes the status of the individual.

**Citizenship (cf.)** is the highest status in this regard, with modern citizens usually equally enjoying the full set of rights guaranteed by their constitution, or charter, or similar document. In return, citizens will also bear certain responsibilities and duties towards their state. **Permanent Residence (cf.)** usually follows, which has many but not all of the rights and duties of citizenship associated with it. Various forms of temporary or precarious immigration status have differential sets of rights to a lesser degree. **Refugees (cf.)** and **Refugee Claimants (cf.)** fall into this category, with their rights respected only insofar as the governing state of the country where they find themselves chooses to abide by their international and national **Legislation (cf.)**, which determine the rights of refugees.

Refugee Status Determination (RSD) is a lengthy, quasi-judicial, and bureaucratic process, requiring a great amount of expertise, to determine whether individuals claiming refuge and seeking asylum are indeed "refugees" in that they meet the conditions of the **1951 Refugee Convention (cf.)**. In Canada, the crucial **Hearing (cf.)** is a form of Refugee Status Determination. A refugee who has an accepted claim can look forward to leaving their temporary status behind and attaining a new, more desirable and stable status—although not without facing further administrative **Barriers (cf.)** along the way.

Although being "status poor" is an unstable and degrading situation, where constant advocacy **(cf. Activism & Advocacy)** is needed to achieve basic rights, statelessness **(cf. Statelessness & State Protection)** and having no status at all is worse. The condition of "naked" or "bare" humanity, where the state recognizes no form of obligation towards a person, leaves them in a fully vulnerable situation where none of their basic **Human Rights (cf.)** are guaranteed. It is not surprising then that at key moments in modern history, states have formally stripped citizens of their nationality and citizenship, rendering them stateless, before proceeding to commit the gravest atrocities against them.

# traf·fick·ing

## Shiva Nourpanah

Human trafficking is a dreadful crime, and indeed may be considered a form of modern slavery. It involves the forcible removal of people from their homes to other places, usually for the purposes of exploitative labour. It may involve a form of deception or fraud. Unlike **Smuggling (cf.)**, which is usually conceptualized as a business transaction between two willing adults, in trafficking there may be a long-lasting relationship between the trafficker and their victims, and a toxic power imbalance between them. Victims may be told that they have no option but to work for their traffickers in order to pay off debts incurred by the cost of their movements. Traffickers generally target children, women, and poor, racialized or marginalized people with little or no access to assistance and support **(cf. Gender and Vulnerability & Resiliency)**. In some instances, poorer families are known to arrange for the trafficking of their children, sometimes to work in the homes or businesses of wealthier relatives. Reliable statistics on the magnitude and numbers of victims and the profits derived from them are scant, however the consensus is that trafficking and modern slavery are flourishing businesses.

It is a myth, and a harmful one at that, that trafficking usually takes place in relation to the sex trade and prostitution. North American policies to combat trafficking generally target the sex trade—something which activists argue may lead to the greater victimization of prostitutes. In fact, most trafficking involves the movement of labourers to work in the "underground" or "black" market under exploitative and abusive circumstances. The work ranges from domestic, agricultural, and factory work, to low-level service provision, for example in beauty salons and parlours. Wealthier societies seem comfortable with the fact that their consumables are mostly produced, and a range of their low-level services provided, by people working in cruel and intolerable if invisible conditions. Until we have the political will to change the conditions in which trafficking flourishes, it seems safe to predict that this heinous crime will continue unabated.

# un·ac·com·pa·nied mi·nors

## Catherine Bryan

Unaccompanied Refugee Children and/or Minors (URMS) is the title commonly used by policymakers, **UNHCR (cf.)**, and within the academic literature to signal children and/or minors who seek asylum independently of a parent or other adult who is socially, culturally, or otherwise deemed responsible for them. Over the last several decades, there has been a growth in the number of unaccompanied minors seeking **Asylum (cf.)** globally. Relative to their adult counterparts, unaccompanied minors face a number of additional **Barriers (cf.)**, including a heightened risk of **Trafficking (cf.)** and exploitation, and difficulties in accessing state protection. Moreover, although they are children, unaccompanied minors remain vulnerable to anti-refugee discourse regarding criminality, illegal entry, and welfare dependency, and as such may experience challenges during resettlement in host communities **(cf. Vulnerability & Resiliency)**. That said, despite the presence of barriers and challenges, unaccompanied minors often demonstrate considerable skill and ability in navigating these conditions.

# U

## UNHCR
### United Nations High Commissioner for Refugees

## Shiva Nourpanah

UNHCR, also known as the UN Refugee Agency, was initially established in 1950 to protect and support those refugees left in the devastating aftermath of the Second World War. It is charged with overseeing the implementation of the **1951 Refugee Convention (cf.)** and currently has offices in 130 countries globally. UNHCR partners with governments and local and international NGOs, such as the International Organization for Migration (IOM), to provide services to refugees. Depending on the context and the situation of refugees, these services may range from the provision of life-saving essentials in the immediate aftermath of conflict to longer-term solutions such as **Repatriation (cf.)** or **Resettlement (cf.)** and macro-level strategizing about the global plight of refugees.

UNHCR has received the Nobel Peace Prize twice for the services it has rendered to refugees, and offers its own prize, the prestigious annual Nansen Refugee Award, to recognize outstanding service to the cause of refugees, displaced, or stateless people. "The Canadian people"[38] were honoured by

---

[38] As written on the award.

receiving the Nansen Refugee Award in 1986 for their welcoming reception of Vietnamese refugees.

Despite the undoubted service of UNHCR to the cause of refugees at both the global and local level, its operations are not beyond criticism. UNHCR staff members have been accused of corruption on many different occasions—a fact that is reflective of the extreme imbalance of power that exists between officers (who have the ability to make life-or-death decisions for refugees) and the vulnerable populations whom they serve. Moreover, the presence of UNHCR, representing as it does the international community and bringing desirable Western cash and goods into impoverished and conflict-ridden communities, has been seen to distort and skew local relations, and breed resentment and hostility. NGOs that depend on UNHCR funding to conduct vital operations also complain of unfavourable political dynamics in their relationships with this huge agency, and a lack of true collaboration and consultation in their joint projects. At the other end of the spectrum, national governments accuse UNHCR of meddling in their internal affairs and their handling of unwanted foreigners. Many academics and refugee activists consider large agencies such as UNHCR as too unwieldy and politicized to bring about real, lasting change in refugee affairs.

Although UNHCR is supposed to maintain an officially neutral stance in conflict, UNHCR aid-workers have themselves become the unfortunate targets of military activities hostile to Western interests. For example, the bomb attack against UNHCR offices in Baghdad in 2003 left at least eighteen staff dead. Such attacks serve as a reminder that that aid work conducted with even the loftiest and most humane objectives is inevitably politicized, and that refugee work in particular can never be free from political associations.

vul·ner·a·bil·i·ty
& re·sil·i·en·cy

# Yanery Navarro Vigil

Most English dictionaries define "resilience" as the quality to recover from something. Most English dictionaries define "vulnerability" as the quality of being exposed to something. Probably, these two concepts are brothers—or even twins—working in tandem in our everyday lives. On a regular basis, we wake up vulnerable and fall asleep resilient. We can be resilient only because we are always already vulnerable.

Our stability is susceptible to different environmental factors. Migration is a prototypical form of vulnerability and resilience. **Forced Migration (cf.)** is the paradigmatic destabilizer. Being a refugee, an asylum seeker, a prisoner, a trafficked person, an undocumented traveller, or any other person with a precarious, limbic status **(cf. Limbo)** that deprives one of stability, entails being in processes in which the balance of these two qualities, resilience and vulnerability, is broken under the collapse of everything familiar.

Yet as a **Refugee (cf.)**, in a state of crisis, one must master the interplay of these sensations in order to survive. How to do that?

In a **Hearing (cf.)**, for example, (an experience much like a criminal's experience in an interrogation room), refugees are expected to express their vulnerabilities in relation to the **Persecution (cf.)** they are fleeing from. They have to prove themselves vulnerable to the point of helplessness, while at the same time they are expected to show resilience so as to be considered a person who will be able to build a life and integrate in the society that they are asking to accept them.

war

# Amara Bangura

Escaping bullets in conflict zones is not a choice; it's a must! I was a teenager when the rebels attacked my town in Sierra Leone. Like many others, I ran to the bushes to escape the rebel slaughter, but I could not run away from hunger, heavy winds, snakes, and wild animals. The terrible weather conditions often forced me to return home for shelter and face the rebels who were high on drugs and armed with all sorts of weapons.

But forget about me and for a second think of the children, the physically challenged, and the mentally ill who could not make the crucial decisions that I made to survive. How did they survive the war? Pa Tik Daddy, my neighbour, was visually impaired and he knew that the rebels would show no mercy should they find him in town. He also knew that a flying bullet does not choose who to kill. So he fled the town a day before the rebels attacked us, and for three days and nights he helplessly wandered; he struggled through bushes, crossed running streams, and hid in a forest, where he was rescued by a family that had also fled the town. He arrived with bruises all over his body, cold, and traumatized.

But after much support from fellow displaced villagers, Pa Tik was relieved that he had been able to escape the bullet.

The circumstances and challenges faced by Pa Tik Daddy are the everyday reality of many refugees crossing international borders to find safety. The situation that awaits them when they land in safe countries is unknown. They hope for an easy integration process, but that's often not the case. There are social pressures in safe cities that make their situation difficult. A young man from Congo opened up to me: "People think I am weird, they laugh at whatever I do, it makes me feel uncomfortable."

I understand what he meant because I have been through similar situations. At a pub in downtown Halifax, a lady, probably in her fifties, laughed just after I introduced myself as a Sierra Leonean. The only thing she knew about my country was of the war that ended over fifteen years ago. With a broad smile on her face she questioned me: "Were you a fighter?" "Nope," I replied. And I quickly drank my beer and left. Questions like this are hard to answer, especially when they come with a smile. It shuts every door to a civilized conversation. Despite the economic incentives, health care, and other social opportunities that encourage refugees to stay, a country's citizens laughing about their situation and describing them as "war victims" instead of survivors is a heavy burden to bear.

## Fadi Hamdan &
## Kathryn Bates-Khan

Youth who are refugees may have experienced interrupted or lost schooling, endured war, or lived through traumatic events and had no choice about leaving their countries and coming to Canada. Refugee youth are entering the settlement process at a time when their emotional and physical development is already in upheaval. The challenges of language barriers, racism, balancing cultural identities, parental conflict, academic success, isolation, and shifting familial roles are further compounded by occurring at a point in time when their sense of identity, relationships with others, and views of the world are being formed in the most basic ways. It is important to recognize that youth have unique settlement needs that are different from adults. Some protective factors that support successful integration include positive school experiences, strong and healthy family relationships, and access to activities and programs that build a sense of belonging to the surrounding community.

# youth & sec·ond gen·er·a·tion

## Morgan Poteet

The term "refugee youth" refers to a subgroup of the wider refugee population with variable upper and lower age cut-offs. Refugee youth share experiences with non-refugee youth and with refugee adults, but their collective experiences are distinct from both. They are, at least initially, at a disadvantage at school, both socially and academically, relative to their Canadian-born peers—and yet they are also "resettlement champions" who typically learn the dominant language and acculturate more quickly than their parents.[39]

The term "second generation" (the members of which are also referred to as the "children of refugees") further distinguishes those born in a reception country from their parents' generation, who arrived as refugees. While cultural identity for the first generation is rooted in their **Country of Origin (cf.)**, the second generation often combines elements of their cultural background with the dominant culture in which they live. Furthermore, on

---

[39]Michaela Hynie, Sepali Guruge, and Yogendra B. Shakya, "Family Relationships of Afghan, Karen and Sudanese Refugee Youth," *Canadian Ethnic Studies/Études Ethniques au Canada*, 44, no. 3 (2012): 11–28.

average, they tend to surpass the levels of education of both their parents and their Canadian-born peers.[40]

The children of refugees who arrive in a reception country at a young age are sometimes referred to as the "1.5 generation," and the younger their age at arrival, the more closely their experiences in the reception country tend to resemble those of the second generation. While the term "second generation" has been widely adopted by scholars to refer to the children of immigrants born in a reception country, the use of the term specifically for the children of refugees is more controversial. Using the term risks prolonging the attachment of the label of "refugee" to the next generation, and is therefore less common. Paradoxically, it also raises awareness about a population that defines their identities and sense of belonging in ways that are distinct from those of the first generation.

---

[40]Childs, Stephen, Ross Finnie, and Richard E. Mueller, "Why Do So Many Children of Immigrants Attend University? Evidence for Canada," *Journal of International Migration & Integration*, 18, no. 1 (2017): 1–28

# Contributor Biographies

## Editors

**Catherine Baillie Abidi** is a scholarly practitioner who bridges community and academia. She has twenty years experience working in the humanitarian field, particularly in the areas of forced migration, peace and conflict, and refugee settlement. She holds a PhD (2015) in educational studies from St. Francis Xavier University in Antigonish, Nova Scotia, Canada, and has published work on refugee settlement and policies in Atlantic Canada, migration and gender, and the changing landscape of political discourse on forced migration. Catherine has led many community-based programs focused on settlement and integration, including creating a refugee-centred storytelling program and a Girl Guide unit specifically organized for girls with refugee backgrounds.

**Shiva Nourpanah** holds a PhD in social anthropology from Dalhousie University, Halifax, Canada. Her areas of research include the experiences of refugees and temporary migrants in Nova Scotia. Formerly, she worked for eight years in Iran with refugees as a staff-member of the United Nations High Commissioner for Refugees (UNHCR). She has published work on the ethics of refugee aid, women's human rights in refugee aid, and the experiences of settlement and integration of Afghan refugees in Halifax. Currently, she is researching the role of sexual and gender-based violence in refugee claims. She has been a member of the Board of Directors of the Halifax Refugee Clinic.

# Contributors

**Benjamin Amaya** was born in El Salvador, and has studied cultural anthropology in Costa Rica, Calgary, and Quebec City. He has conducted research on identity and social life among youth in Central America and Canada. He currently teaches at Dalhousie University in Halifax, Canada.

**Amara Bangura** is a Sierra Leonean journalist based in Halifax with more than fifteen years of experience reporting and producing programs for international media organizations such as the BBC and Journalists for Human Rights. He holds a master's degree in media and international development from the University of East Anglia, UK, and is also a recipient of the prestigious Gordon N. Fisher/JHR Journalism Fellowship at Massey College, University of Toronto.

**Kathryn Bates-Khan** is an educator and lifelong learner committed to social justice and human rights. During her career at YMCA, she has led multiple programs for immigrant children and youth and is currently leading the Halifax YMCA's Gender-based Violence Prevention Project.

**Catherine Bryan** is a social anthropologist and professor of social work at Dalhousie University in Halifax, Canada. Her research focuses on political economy, social reproduction, and migration.

**Sylvia Calatayud** has a master's degree in adult education from Mount Saint Vincent University in Halifax and a master's in art therapy from Kutenai Art Therapy Institute in Nelson, British Columbia. She is a consultant and facilitator of workshops around diversity and inclusion, cultural humility, immigration, and art-based research.

**Julie Chamagne** has been the executive director of Halifax Refugee Clinic for over a decade. She received legal training in France and the UK, and has worked in asylum law overseas. She has been an advocate for migrant and refugee rights for the past twenty years.

**Marianela Fuertes** is an international human rights lawyer, former auxiliary judge of the Supreme Court of Colombia, and a former restorative justice caseworker.

**Pauline Gardiner Barber** is a professor in the Department of Sociology and Social Anthropology at Dalhousie University. Her publications and teaching encompass global migration and citizenship issues with a special emphasis on the Philippines and how migration is reshaping Filipino lives and livelihoods.

**Wenche Gausdal** is the director of programs, settlement, community integration & support services at Immigrant Services Association of Nova Scotia (ISANS). She has a master's degree in social work from Dalhousie University and is registered with the Nova Scotia College of Social Workers. Throughout her twenty-two year career with ISANS, Wenche has helped to resettle over seven thousand refugees.

**Fadi Hamdan** is the YMCA manager of child & youth settlement and advisor for the national COA Youth Refugee Program, which provides pre-arrival services for youth overseas. These work experiences, in conjunction with representation on multiple community boards and committees, have contributed to his own commitment and passion for engaging youth and community in meaningful ways that promote shared growth and learning.

**Josh Judah**, QC, is the chief prosecutor with the Halifax Regional Municipality. As a volunteer, he is the Associate General Counsel with the Halifax Refugee Clinic and has been representing refugee claimants for two decades.

**Sara Mahaney** is a practising lawyer in Halifax, Nova Scotia. She has provided pro bono legal representation to refugee claimants and is a member of the Halifax Refugee Clinic's Board of Directors.

**Huwaida Medani** is an educator and diversity and inclusion consultant. She holds a master's degree in educational psychology from the Mount Saint Vincent University, Halifax, Nova Scotia. Huwaida's work focuses on education, community development, diversity, inclusion, and migration.

**Yanery Navarro Vigil** is a doctoral student in Educational Studies at Mount Saint Vincent University. From biological sciences to philosophy, she cultivates her interdisciplinary background with a focus on adult education and refugee studies. She has been volunteering for the past three years with the public library system, mentoring students who, like her, have faced forced migration, in their English through its English as an Additional Language (EAL) program.

**San Patten** is a member of the Board of Directors of the Halifax Refugee Clinic. She is a health research consultant specializing in HIV, drug use, and sexual health, including issues related to migrant health.

**Morgan Poteet** is an associate professor of sociology at Mount Allison University in Sackville, New Brunswick. Poteet's current research explores the subjective experiences of belonging and exclusion of the 1.5 and second generation Central American immigrants and refugees in Ontario.

**Gillian Smith** has been the settlement coordinator at the Halifax Refugee Clinic (HRC) for ten years, and is responsible for leading and developing the HRC's settlement services. She has a background in international development studies and speaks French and Spanish. She is passionate about breaking down barriers and creating more awareness of the challenges people face due to immigration status—and how status is inextricably linked to access to services and inclusion.

**Evangelia (Evie) Tastsoglou**, LLM, PhD, is Professor of Sociology and Coordinator of the International Development Studies Program at Saint Mary's University in Halifax. With sociological and legal training, she has over twenty-five years of expertise in working with gender and other various aspects of international migration and Canadian immigration and integration. She is currently researching sexual and gender-based violence and precarity during forced migration, with focus on journeys through the eastern Mediterranean.

**Katie Tinker** worked as Legal Case Manager with the Halifax Refugee Clinic between 2012 and 2018. During this time she assisted many clients with the process of applying for refugee protection in Canada. Katie holds a master's degree in development economics from Dalhousie University, and she continues to volunteer her time in support of refugees and refugee claimants.

# Photography Credits